LIFE
BETWEEN
HEAVEN
AND
EARTH

GEORGE
ANDERSON

AND

ANDREW
BARONE

LIFE
BETWEEN
HEAVEN
AND
EARTH

What You Didn't Know
About the World Hereafter
and How It Can Help You

 HARMONY

BOOKS · NEW YORK

Published in the United States by Harmony Books, an imprint of the
Crown Publishing Group, a division of Penguin Random House LLC,
New York.
crownpublishing.com

Harmony Books is a registered trademark, and the Circle colophon is a
trademark of Penguin Random House LLC.

Library of Congress Cataloging-in-Publication Data is available upon
request.

ISBN 978-0-553-41949-8
eBook ISBN 978-0-553-41950-4

Printed in the United States of America

Jacket design by Jenny Carrow
Jacket photograph by Philip and Karen Smith/Getty Images

10 9 8 7 6 5 4 3 2 1

First Edition

This book is dedicated to the memory of
Theresa Runyon—aunt, mentor, and friend.
—GEORGE ANDERSON

This book is also dedicated with love and gratitude to
Chelsea Richard, my angel in heaven,
and
Brian Rothschild, my angel on earth.
—ANDREW BARONE

Contents

LIFE

BETWEEN

HEAVEN

AND

EARTH

Prologue

THE DOORS OF HEAVEN AND EARTH

Whoever coined the phrase "There's nothing new under the sun" has never encountered the souls of the world hereafter. Neither has that person likely benefited in any tangible way from the extraordinary point of view only the souls can provide. Every day that the sun rises, the souls have their hands and their hearts in our world— helping to shape the circumstances of our lives, and showing us new and unique ways to understand both our world and theirs. After almost fifty years as a medium and a lifetime of listening to the souls speak of the vagaries of heaven and earth, I am still learning that when it comes to the world hereafter, there will *always* be something new under the sun.

This book is something a little different for us, and definitely something new in my communication with the world hereafter. It's the story of some of the more unique circumstances of living and dying on the earth, and how the souls are able to change our lives and experiences in a way that will bring about the best resolution of our life lessons—even in what may seem to be some rather impossible circumstances. This is a book about the souls at their most creative, their most ingenious, and their most caring at the critical time we find ourselves struggling to find a method to the madness of our lives. These stories help us to understand that no matter what happens, here or in the hereafter, there will be a way to move us through the doors of heaven and earth so that we may realize, complete, and conquer our spiritual journey.

This is the year I've decided to come to a certain peace about two undeniable facts of my existence on the earth: I am a man of advancing age, and in my advancing age I have become my father. I catch myself saying, "*In my day . . .*" and "*You kids have no idea*" as reflexive responses to something I'm unfamiliar with or to which I cannot relate. Like computers. And cell phones. I am now, without any reservation, a man who can safely be categorized as "from an-other generation," and I've found that fighting it is a fool's game. But with advancing age comes some wisdom. It took me a long time to understand why I inexplicably wake up at the crack of dawn and stare intensely at the rising sun, and why I stop in my tracks at the end of the day to watch the sun in its last brilliant minutes on our plane. At first I thought my *stop, stand, and muse* was a learned behavior—my father was famous in our family for doing exactly the same thing. But now that I am comfortably "of a certain age," I'm starting to realize that there is perhaps meaning to these actions. And that there are secrets unknown to us until they are revealed by the universe, secrets that teach us a thing or two about our world. So this man from another generation has come to a rather amazing understanding of life that perhaps cannot be seen by *this* generation of young, but restless eyes, or understood by the fresh, but occupied mind. It is a message both simple and profound—we live the most when the light first illuminates our lives, and we learn the most in the moments of twilight as we cling to the last moments of fading light. Come heaven or earth, come life here or life hereafter, ours is a world lived entirely between two doors.

From a very young age, I've been given an insight into the portals that exist between our world and the next from the souls who reached out to me after a childhood illness nearly took my life. At the age of six, after catching chicken pox, I quickly developed a nearly fatal case of encephalomyelitis—a swelling of the brain. Though I did recover, I lost the use of my legs for about three months, and had to learn to crawl around the house when I wasn't remanded to my bed by my Irish Catholic mother, who believed to the day she passed that her unshakeable, unwavering faith kept me from dying. But what she didn't expect that unwavering faith to subsequently do was have part of my damaged brain overrepair itself to the point that it became a kind of shortwave radio, allowing the souls to communicate to me.

As I was learning to walk again, I started seeing images and hearing voices. Some came with a certain sense of familiarity about them—relatives—but mostly the voices and images belonged to people I did not know. The most frequent visitor who came to me was the figure of a woman I called "Lilac Lady" because of her lilac-colored robes, who I later came to understand was St. Joan of Arc. As a young girl in the thirteenth century, *Jeanne d'Arc*, as she was known, received visions from the Archangel Michael, and used her ability to communicate with the souls in order to help Charles VII and France win victory from English domination. But in spite of her divine journey, she was ultimately convicted of a variety of offenses by a French Bishop who still maintained English loyalty. She was ordered to be burned at the stake at the age of nineteen. Joan (and I'm sure she'll forgive my informality as we've been friends for some fifty-five years) was, like me, the youngest child in her family, and also like me, began hearing voices and seeing figures at a very young age. As I got older, however, I found out, just as she did, what kind of liability seeing and hearing the souls could be for someone so young. Like Joan, I was persecuted by those around me, and also thought to be insane. But I know that even after she helped save me from fatal illness, she again stepped in and helped save my life.

At about the same age that Joan met her death, I was being brought to the now defunct Pilgrim State Hospital, a psychiatric facility on Long Island, where the doctors diagnosed me with schizophrenia. It was only by the kindness of one doctor, and the encouragement and extraordinary influence of Joan, that I wasn't left to rot in that facility. In many ways, I believe Joan chose me as an ally and has remained a constant presence in my life because we share the same ideal—that communication with the souls is *not* a gift, but an ability we were given, a life commitment, and a responsibility to the world of Light, that we must use to the best of our ability to help bring peace and understanding to the world.

I understand that my life's work as a medium is a tool I must use to bring messages of comfort, hope, and peace to people on this plane who struggle to understand, who need to learn, and who need to find hope. I have been able to grow and move from period to period in my life—from natural curiosity about my ability to abject hostility toward it due to fear, then to understanding my vocation in life as a communicator for the souls, and finally to these years of coming to clearer understanding about the souls and their messages. And the souls use me as an instrument to communicate their incredible messages for a very good reason: they want to inspire each of us in enough ways that we can then go on, enriched by their knowledge, and inspire the world.

As the years go on, I find that the souls are revealing more information about the complex issues we face in our world, and some of the more delicate circumstances they face in theirs. I'm hearing more often in sessions that contrary to what we may think, there really are no absolutes in life here *or* hereafter—things change, people change, circumstances change, and even the souls change with their own spiritual growth, our prayers, and communication to and from the earth. As they've trusted me more, they've told me more. And as I've grown, so have the insights the souls can provide—they've come to acknowledge that life sometimes beats the starch out of the most tenuous of our beliefs, and that our existence is not always so much black and white as it is a series of different degrees of light. This is where the souls have been "living" lately in my perspective and in my own growth as a medium— they seem now, more than at any other time in my life, to want to tell us more about their extraordinary world so that we can better understand our own.

We live and die sometimes under the most preposterous of circumstances. We can't always expect things to be packaged up as neatly as we believe they should be when the story ends. Unusual situations that arise on our journey—and beyond—require creative, thoughtful, and sometimes *unusual* solutions. Some roads to peace may need a little more navigation than others. Some struggles in life may need special attention. Some resolutions, both here and hereafter, may take some time, resourcefulness, and patience. If you are surprised that it all isn't quite as tidy as you thought it would be, then join the club—it took me sixty-odd years of life to understand it myself. But the gist of the story of our world, our life, and our universe is this: it's *moveable,* and sometimes the universe needs to move *with* us to bring peace and resolution to our lives and our world. Is this something new? I don't think so. What I can tell you is that it's news to *me,* and a real evolution of thought and education. This is where I find myself with the souls, and this is why, with the souls' nudging, we have written another book. The souls need us to listen carefully to what they have to say. They want to tell us what they have learned about our world, now that they can see it in all dimensions and with perfect clarity. They know our lives are complicated, and they know that the journey is not always easy. But they also know that happy resolutions to the complexities of life, even those that may defy explanation, are not only possible—they can be quite amazing.

After so many years of hearing from the souls and decades of listening to stories of life both here and hereafter, I can tell you without reservation that there is an answer to every question, a solution to every problem, and a completion of everything left unfinished in our lives. The manner in which that happens, however, is what makes the souls' world so extraordinary. The souls can help make perfect any circumstance in a world that seems sometimes to teeter on the brink of complete chaos. But it seems that only lately have they begun to trust us to understand the fact that even in their world perfection is relative. It sometimes needs a little finesse. And this seems to be the time in our lives that they want us to know. The souls have been speaking with absolute honesty about how perfect resolutions are possible, even in imperfect lives and circumstances. And once again, through the stories of ordinary people who have had extraordinary experiences in life and death, they are able to demonstrate the beauty of this concept in spectacular fashion.

As the souls communicate more about their lives, I understand more clearly that our entire existence here sits at the center hub of a wheel of doors. From very early on in my career I've known the importance of *doors* with regard to the souls and our lives—they've mentioned the portal that leads from their world to ours when our journey begins on the earth, and the portal that opens and welcomes us back when it is our time to leave the earth. But between these portals, there are doors that open inward to allow people and circumstances into our lives, and doors that swing outward to allow people to leave and follow their own destiny. There are doors we may slip through unexpectedly, and doors our fate will push us through for our own good. Though each is different and some are challenging, they all lead eventually to the peace, joy, and understanding of the world hereafter.

The reference to *walking from one room to another* that the souls use so often to describe the movement between our world and theirs is an important allegory. They want us to understand that nothing is ever static in life here or hereafter, and that we have to allow the doors to open and close at the times they have to. But in the last few years, the souls have also tried to expand our understanding by showing in sessions how these doors will also shift and move for us when they *need* to. We only need to wait and allow the right door to find us. In effect, the doors of our existence move around us, as if on a wheel, until the intended life circumstance presents itself. If the door stops in front of us, we must walk through it—it was meant for us, no matter how random that choice may seem at the time. There is a plan in place, and in order to keep us moving forward to the fulfillment of our destiny, the doors will continue to move until the right one leads us through the journey of our lives.

What has been the most significant revelation for me in my work recently is the understanding that on this wheel of doors, according to the souls, there is a wildcard—an *other* door—one that an unusual or complicated circumstance creates a need for, to make it possible for them to change the course of our journey. It's not very common, but when it happens, it's for a very important reason— the souls need a way to help us back on track so that we may complete the story of our life. The souls know that sometimes life for us will veer off its intended path. They know that when things have gone wrong, something extraordinary will need to happen in order to place us back where we need to be to complete our spiritual journey. *Happy endings* can always be found in the world hereafter, though sometimes the method of getting us to our place of peace may be a little unusual.

The stories in this book represent times, both on the earth and in the hereafter, when unusual circumstances make it necessary to find an alternate path—for another door to open. The stories are compelling, and even a bit surprising, but they represent how nothing is impossible in our life between heaven and earth. Just as we are unique in this world, so, too, is the journey we are on, and the resolution we will fashion from whatever we face in our lives. The reason for the bend in the path will eventually make itself known. It will help resolve the struggle to find perspective on what may sometimes seem to be the chaos of a life unresolved, a journey mis-understood, or a life lesson unvalued. In other words, in time, the imperfect becomes perfected with a little help from the hereafter.

The people whose stories and sessions appear in this book are real—they live on the earth and in the hereafter, and, except where names have been changed to respect their privacy, nothing in their stories has been altered. Some are difficult to imagine and others are heartbreaking to read, but they are all *beautiful*—they are poi-gnant reminders about the strength of the human soul, and they tell the most accurate story yet of the amazing ways our universe can accommodate, shift, move, and morph into whatever we need to attain resolution and peace in the hereafter.

In our sessions, I was in charge of speaking to the souls, and did not know the circumstances or the people attending the session until the minute the session started. My coauthor, Andrew, worked with the sitters independent of the sessions to learn their reasons for attending the session, and to chronicle their stories and those of their loved ones. We did not come together again until all the sessions were done so that each of us would have no knowledge of the other's work. In this book the sitters' stories are followed by the sessions.

It is with profound gratitude to each of these brave, generous families that we are able to present another facet in what we con-sider a perfect diamond: the grace and peace of the world hereafter.

We hope you find insight and inspiration in the words of both the families and the souls. The souls knew at the time that they were not only speaking to me but to all of us. They were anxious that those of us on earth learn, understand, and grow in comfort and peace, just as the souls do.

As always, through more than half a century of communication, I am grateful to the souls for their kindness, for their ability to educate us, and for inspiring each of us to continue learning and growing until we see them again in their beautiful world. We sincerely hope you feel the same.

1

THE REVELATION

PEGGY AND DENIS O'CONNOR

Just a few minutes before we were to meet, I was told the subjects of this session were Elaine and Joe Stillwell. It was a nice surprise, since I hadn't seen them for a few years. It would be nice to get caught up, I thought.

As I stood to go to the conference room door to greet them in advance of their arrival, my thoughts immediately went to the chairs—comfy, swiveling, leather armchairs that I can, and have, sat in for hours. I knew Elaine and Joe would get a kick out of the chairs. Many things had changed over the many years since I started working in earnest out of my house in Deer Park, Long Island, after taking a chance and leaving my job as an operator at the New York Telephone Company, including the furnishings. More than thirty years ago, Elaine and Joe had come to a small group session held in my home. Money was tight, so things were as basic as you could get. The room in which I held sessions was unfurnished, except for a framed print of a schooner (which the home's previous owners had left hanging in order to avoid having to repaint the wall that had faded around it), a table lamp that gave off a hideous glare, and the beat-up armchair in which I sat. My clients sat on borrowed folding chairs, sometimes for hours, to hear from their loved ones and to reconnect with the souls they had lost. The leather chairs were certainly an upgrade.

At our first meeting more than thirty years ago, I realized I already "knew" Elaine and Joe, without ever having met them before. I remembered reading in the paper about a terrible accident in which two young people, a brother and sister, lost their lives. They were driving back from a concert at the Jones Beach Theater when they attempted to cross a small drawbridge. They must not have realized that the single flashing light on that darkened road meant the bridge was on its way up. Their car hit the rising portion of the bridge, killing one sibling. The other, who was critically injured, died four days later at the hospital.

The story resonated with me because I knew the area where they were killed. During the day, it's a beautiful sun-soaked drive through dunes and gorgeous water views. But at night, that beautiful ride becomes a daunting labyrinth of dark stretches and sudden turns on a poorly lit highway. It always surprised me that more people didn't meet tragedy driving through that desolate area at night.

The siblings were Elaine's children from her first marriage. The souls identified themselves in the session as Denis and Margaret, a formal name the young lady quickly changed to Peggy. They talked about their closeness and an unusually deep friendship for sister and brother. They insisted that although the bridge was poorly lit and the drawbridge signal nearly impossible to see, the accident was nobody's fault. But then, Denis, the older of the two, said something extraordinary that made me sit up straight in my chair. He told us that Peggy had died instantly in the crash, but he had lingered. He explained that while he was in a coma, Peggy came to tell him that she had passed on, that she was going ahead of him to the hereafter. Denis, fearing not only that he could never live with the pain of losing his sister but also that he would have to bear the responsibility for her passing, decided that he wanted to go with her. After clinging to life for three days, Denis passed, following his sister into a world of joy.

I was young at the time, still in my thirties, and it was the first time in hundreds of sessions that any of the souls had dared to tell me they had a choice: to stay on the earth or go on to the hereafter. It took me a second to comprehend what was being said. Although the souls had told me many times that there is a day and an hour we will pass on, sometimes it is possible to rewrite the script, to bend the rules, to literally change what I had been taught by the souls was a one-way ride. In the past, the souls had been very resolute on this point. We live, we pass on, we continue forward to the hereafter on a specific day and at a specific time. It all seemed so tidy. But this new information generated more questions than it answered, especially for me. Is fixing what dumb luck seems to have broken something the souls are able to do? What about the life journey? Wasn't that plan etched into us even before we were born? It was simple, Denis told me. They weren't rewriting their lives, they were just moving the goalposts a little to bring each other peace, while also still providing the life lesson for those left on the earth.

I almost thought this information would be too much for Elaine to bear. I thought she would cry out at the injustice of losing *two* children simply because it was an easier road for Denis to walk. I looked into her soft eyes, and all I saw was peace. She knew. As a mother, she knew it had been as it had had to be. She told me afterward that that was Denis's way, and that, although it was painful to know his life could have been spared, she understood his decision to go on with his sister and loved him all the more for it.

So I had found out that *choice* is a wild card, and *circumstance* is apparently moveable when the souls need it to be. This was news to me, and a bit of a wrinkle in my thoughts. The souls had usually been straightforward when it came to why we live, why we die, and what we are to learn in both circumstances. But this became one of several asterisks in their narrative, a new concept: that the souls, due to our needs or theirs, can change the journey for us here *or* change the resolution for us in the hereafter simply because there is a greater good at stake. It was a real learning experience for me as well as for the Stillwells, and something that has helped bond us as friends for many years.

When we began writing this book, I tried to think of the times in which the circumstances in sessions were somewhat extraordinary and challenged what we had learned or been told about life here and hereafter. This was the first time I realized that, between these worlds, *anything* is possible for the souls to experience what they need to, so that they can proceed on their own life's journey; and *everything* is possible when you are dealing with the interface between our world and theirs.

Some thirty years had passed since I first met the Stillwells and heard Denis's incredible revelation. We thought it would be interesting to bring Denis and Peggy back and see if their original assessment of their lives and their journey held true, and if, perhaps, they had any nuances they could share with us. To me, the session that follows shows how much they had evolved in their own soul growth as well as how much they were continuing to impact Elaine's and Joe's growth here on the earth.

This is Elaine and Joe's story, in their words:

An incredible journey opened to me following the tragic, sudden deaths of my two oldest children, twenty-one-year-old Denis and nineteen-year-old Peggy, in a car accident on a rainy summer night, August 2, 1986. Peggy died instantly and Denis died four days later, following brain surgery, the day after we buried Peggy. Even in my state of shock and fighting the utter weariness and agony that assaulted my body, I was consumed with a passionate energy to tell the world how much I loved these children. I poured my heart and soul into preparing their funerals and writing their eulogies with every ounce of strength I could muster, thinking that would be my last gift of love to them. As the last guest and all our caretakers left after Denis's funeral, my husband, Joe (stepfather to my children), and I sat there in the living room, staring at each other, thinking, Where do we go from here? How do we get up in the morning? How do we sit at the table with two vacant seats, soon to be three when my remaining child, Annie, leaves to begin her freshman year at college? How do we bear the utter quietness in our house after living with the constant din of telephone calls, stereos, and chatter? How do we face the world again? These were all frightening, overwhelming, almost paralyzing thoughts in those dark first moments of unimaginable grief. I didn't have a clue or a plan for how to survive, but unbeknownst to me, God did.

Peggy and Denis were just a year and a half apart in age, and only separated by a year in school. From the playpen up they were always together and enjoyed the same neighborhood pals and school friends, becoming the "Inseparable Duo." Denis, the first-born, the big brother, the only son, named after his father and grandfather, curly blond hair, piercing green eyes, sunburned nose, and infectious smile; he made his own mold. Social studies, history, the Civil War, Germany, English literature, cooking, and concerts were his special interests. Fishing, surfing, skiing, and camping fed his love of the outdoors. Swimming, soccer, baseball, and lacrosse filled his life with that competitive zest. But music was his spirit! He had a charm that could move all ages, a wit that could keep you entertained for hours, a smile that could not be forgotten, and a love of life that would make you feel how great it was to be young. He had belonged to the fraternity of lifeguards since he was sixteen, risking his life for others every day. And this giving of self was evidenced in the very last act of his life: the donation of his organs to save or better the lives of others. Friends were his anchors, Samantha was his love, Peggy was his pal, and Annie was the one he loved to tease.

Denis loved life, being on the go, traveling, getting together with friends, talking till the wee hours of the morning. He was a loyal fan of football pools, the Mets, the Islanders, Notre Dame, and the horse "My Boy Dennis." Surf shirts, crazy hats, and sunglasses were his trademark. He was surrounded with golf clubs, lacrosse sticks, stereo tapes, records, and whatever else he could fit into his car.

Following high school graduation, he took an extra year to knuckle down, get back on track, and apply himself to his studies.

After graduating from Nassau Community College, he was excited and eager to be heading to Northeastern University in Boston a few weeks later, to major in International Relations and pursue their work-study program, "on the eight-year plan," as he called it. After his accident we honestly thought he would recover from brain surgery in time to be there shortly after the semester began, but it was not to be.

Peggy was a beautiful free spirit who enjoyed colorful outfits, dangling jewelry, and big pocketbooks. She truly relished life and loved being Irish. Music and rhythm were part of her vitality. Expressing her thoughts verbally or in writing was her forte, and choosing just the right card to send you was her specialty. She had a knack for expressing exactly how she felt in a concise, humorous style that endeared her to you. She bared her soul to Denis, shared her soul with Annie, and spoiled our dog, Mickey, who was her shadow.

Peggy loved parties, staying up late, baking, shopping, celebrations, Christmas, balloons, crepe paper, and tradition. She was loyal to the core and had an innate sense of fairness. She was a good friend. She made her share of poor choices, but could always say, "I'm sorry." She tested the rules, affected by her father's long-term health issues and her parents' divorce, but got through "teenage syndrome" in one piece. Attending the University of Dayton, living in "The Ghetto" there, being a member of Lambda Nu sorority, deciding on a psychology major were joys to her. Whether babysitting; dog-walking; working at the A&P, Nassau Beach, or the Nassau County Probation Department; or just being your friend, she joked and laughed and made you feel the happiness in her soul. People responded to "Peggy O's" twinkling green eyes, her impish smile, her famous dimple on the chin (devil within), and those unforgettable freckles! None of us will ever forget her sensitive, fragile, beautiful, loving spirit that enhanced our lives. When Peggy died, I immediately comforted myself by believing she was in heaven with my mother, for whom she was named. It made my heart feel so good to know Peggy was not alone and that she was enthusiastically welcomed by my mother. When Denis died, I knew they would both be overjoyed to be reunited, and that notion actually gave me strength to get through the double loss.

Even in my pain, missing them so terribly and surrounded by their possessions, I knew right away that I wanted my children to be proud of me as their mother, living life and not hiding under the covers. I wanted to use that special love I had for them, spread it around and not waste it. I wanted them to be remembered forever, not erased from memory, but I had no clue how that would happen, how they would eventually become known from coast to coast.

In those early days of grief I operated as if by remote control, grateful for my job as a third grade teacher. I returned to work three weeks after burying two of my children because it was the opening of the school year, and you had to be there to set down the rules and the goals for the class to "be yours." It gave me motivation to get up in the morning, structure to my never-ending day, and loving children and colleagues to keep me nurtured, busy, and needed. Little eight-year-olds keep you on your toes all day. I put one foot in front of the other each morning and tried so hard to make sure Peggy and Denis would be proud of me for wanting and trying to have a meaningful life again. When I didn't give homework on Denis's birthday, the children all yelled, "We love

Denis!" How could you beat that? Returning to work was a big door to open.

As months went by, I was bolstered by the books I read, as I eagerly looked for answers to my pain. Learning that others had survived the death of their children gave me inspiration and encouragement for the journey out of the Valley of the Shadow, as they called it. When every book I read mentioned the value of The Compassionate Friends, a national organization for bereaved parents, I was anxious to find such a group near my home, but there was none. So I asked my husband, Joe, if together we could start a local chapter in our hometown. Fourteen months later, in 1987, leaning on each other, we founded The Compassionate Friends (TFC) of Rockville Centre. We held our first meeting on October 9, which happened to be the feast day of Saint Denis. Do you think that was a sign? I did. Definitely another door.

Now I know what you are thinking: How did a newly bereaved parent lead a bereavement group? And you are right. It was the blind leading the blind. Joe and I had as much to learn as every person who came through the door. So what did we do? We ordered a stack of audiotapes from the TCF national office and played them on a boom box as we all listened intently to the message. The tapes dealt with a variety of topics: anger; guilt; communicating with your spouse; dealing with holidays, anniversaries, and birthdays; suicide; sudden death; and more. After listening to a tape, I would use my teaching skills to lead a discussion on the topic of the evening. We all learned how to survive together. Best of all, lifelong friendships were made.

My years of speech and debate in high school and college and three decades of teaching prepared me for sharing my story with a variety of audiences, who practically memorized what I told them. We bonded. They knew I had been there and that I understood their pain—that it was not just book learning that I espoused. I was invited to speak at college courses, churches, seminars, and conferences, and also took part in some of the George Anderson Programs, where I spoke before he appeared to do his readings in seminars. That is how my videotapes (which later became DVDs), *Helping Your Heart Through Grief, Volumes I & II*, were born. They have been shipped all over the United States to newly bereaved parents—including those families who lost a child in Iraq or Afghanistan—by my dear Kentucky friend, Rosemary Smith, another bereaved parent I met along the journey. Rosemary called me after losing her two oldest sons in a car accident similar to the one that took Denis and Peggy. We went on to collaborate on developing bereavement conferences, writing her book, *The Children of the Dome*, and participating in her documentary for bereaved parents, *Space Between Breaths*. One thing just led to another, with many doors swinging open to bring comfort and hope to many lives.

In 1995 I retired from teaching elementary school and planned to write some children's books featuring my dog, Mickey, who was so loved by all the children I had taught over the years. They were thrilled to write or draw pictures of his latest antics for our "Mickey Contests." Not long after, I was invited to be the first bereavement coordinator for the Diocese of Rockville Centre, New York. I didn't want another person to feel the pain that I had endured when there was no help out there to get me through my loss, no support groups available and no follow-up calls or visits from the parish clergy after celebrating two beautiful funerals in one week (no follow-up after the funeral is the second most common complaint of all bereaved persons of all faiths). This invitation was a dream come true, a passionate mission for me. I provided training and enrichment for bereavement ministers in 134 parishes, worked closely with hospitals and counseling agencies, organized bereavement conferences, and answered the inquiries of the bereaved and those trying to help them, opening more doors for everyone.

When families asked how they could get their young children or teens to open up and express their feelings following the death of someone close to them—a grandparent, parent, sibling, friend, or pet—that need inspired me to write two crafts books for grieving children: *Sweet Memories* and *A Forever Angel*. Being creative and making things (alone or with the help of a parent) in memory of their loved one, crafts they would then give to others as a way to remember their special person, often broke the wall of silence and caused children to talk about the person who had died. Another door swung open, bringing comfort to little children and teens.

Following the September 11, 2001, attack on the World Trade Center (only twenty miles from my home), my office was overwhelmed with families to help. The Centering Corporation of Omaha, Nebraska, organized and sent to me $150,000 worth of grief resources (books, CDs, teddy bears) to be distributed to the many families and parishes affected by the tragedy. I opened a distribution center and organized teams of volunteers, and together we delivered these materials all over Long Island.

Four weeks later, I received a call from ACTA Publications in Chicago asking if I would be interested in writing a book to be entitled *The Death of a Child* (they already had published books on coping with the loss of a husband, wife, or parent). I felt I couldn't pass up such a great opportunity, but I was swamped trying to meet the needs of more than five hundred grief-stricken WTC families. How could I find time to write a book, too? Understanding the situation, the publisher asked if he could call me back in three months—and to my delight he really did. I was thrilled, especially when my outline and first chapter were accepted and we signed a contract for one more "dream come true." The first copy, hot off the press, appeared on my doorstep on Christmas Eve 2003, a veritable gift from Santa. No chimney, just another door.

As I reached out to help bereaved families, my life brightened and expanded as "boomerang" rewards came flying my way, bringing new friends, new interests, creative activities, exciting writing opportunities, and a variety of ways to "share Peggy and Denis with the world."

Faithful to our TCF chapter's mantra, "If their song is to continue, then we must do the singing," I am singing loud and clear with my whole heart and soul. Even though Peggy and Denis died in 1986, they are still making a difference in the world today. After years of opening one door after another, building my new life, I believe the ancient words of the teacher and philosopher Hypatia of Alexandria: "Life is an unfoldment, and the further we travel the more truth we can comprehend. To understand the things that are at our door is the best preparation for understanding those that lie beyond."

THE SESSION

(Note: In all the sessions, George Anderson did not know who would be coming to the session or why. In this case, he knew the Stillwells, but he did not know the circumstances under which they were having a session.)

"Okay, let's begin. Don't read between the lines on this—*(to Joe)* . . . a woman comes forward and says she's mom, and she expresses concern with your health. I mean hey, we're not getting any younger, and it stinks getting old. But she's not forecasting that anything horrible is about to happen . . . she just seems to be concerned because you might be stubborn about it. And there's no harm in getting checked. Your two youngsters come forward. In all the times I've done sessions, I don't know if I've ever heard them say this, but they tell me that everything that happens is all part of a huge experience. Hmm. According to your son, you choose to do what you do in this life. And you had to have the experience of loss— otherwise you would not have been able to relate as significantly. And also, your daughter talks about passing—that your son was still in a decision-making zone at the time. But once she passed, he does admit he wanted—not to be insensitive to you, but he says he wanted to go with her."

"Okay."

"He says he wasn't really able to survive and have to experience the *I survived, she didn't* type of mentality, because it's much more difficult to deal with that here. Over there, it's not the case. The two of them are together. They're not only brother and sister but good pals. Soul mates in that sense. It's funny—he does bring up that in another life they were husband and wife. It seems to come up a lot with soul mates and their other connections in other lifetimes.

"But it seems like all of you as a family—before you even came here—kind of sat down and decided on what your experience on the earth was going to be. As your children state, this didn't happen to you because somebody had a bad day over there—you all decided *okay, we're going to do this*—and everybody had their own role to play. This is interesting—I'm not sure if they ever said this to you before, but you definitely had the more difficult part. And you don't need them to tell you that. Nothing to do with religion, but I see Saint Teresa over your head, who brings the virtues of strength, faith, and endurance. She believed that everything is a grace. So in order for you to do to the work that you do with bereaved parents, you had to take their path—you had to experience it. Otherwise you would have been ill-equipped for your journey here. Your son says, in a nice way, that otherwise you'd basically be talking out of your rear end."

(They laugh.) "That's him."

"Everything that goes on in our lives is a grace and has a purpose. Certainly a teacher who teaches history who has experienced some of it is going to be more enthusiastic than somebody who has not. But again—your lives were to run parallel to your children's for the time that they did, and then everything went the way it needed to. Your children say that they know that no matter what you'd rather have them back. You'd rather not be going through this. Your son shows me a carousel—it's like it keeps going in circles. But this was all decided, and it needed to be fulfilled in this lifetime. And it is being fulfilled, because the one thing they both state is that they do admire your perseverance and endurance. And you may basically think that you don't have a choice, but they say it's the right way to look at it—in this regard, this was your spiritual journey, and it was what you had to go through. You're being a realist."

"Yes."

"Interesting—both of them thank you *(to Joe)* because you've been a great support system. You've played a role in this also. You were supposed to come into the picture for a reason, and everybody here has a purpose. Now I know that you've been married before . . . and even that had to happen. They say—it's funny, I keep calling them your *youngsters* but you know what I mean—even with the previous marriage you didn't fail. They've already found out in the hereafter that on earth, there's no such thing as failure. It's an illusion that doesn't exist. It's only something we created here. In your first marriage you had a rough time."

"Yes."

"There was a great deal of unpleasantness from it. They know you bent over backwards trying to make everything right. But it's because we're taught here that if we do a, b, and c, we can expect x, y, and z. But it doesn't always work like that. Both your children know you're much happier now."

"Yes."

"But the main thing here is that you had to go through that. And they had to go through what they did. One thing they do express to me . . . you're obviously a very sensitive individual, and they tell me you've had your times of heavy thought. But your son tells me that he's kind of a referee when that happens—he keeps it in check for you. He gives me the impression that on the earth he could be a real *ball breaker* . . ."

(They laugh.)

". . . and he says he doesn't want you to get the idea he's sprouted wings over there. He says he could be a tough cookie—and he does regret in the past saying the wrong thing at the wrong time—but to him it's all water under the bridge."

"Yes."

"Because even when they passed, you started thinking too much. *Is this a wakeup call? What did I do?* All this wrong thinking that maybe you brought this on yourself . . . but they say that while we're here, we have to experience both the negative and the positive in the people we love—the yin and the yang. Yes, you certainly grow from the positive, but you grow even more from the negative, too. And as they both say—you're not going to be here forever. There's no guarantee we'll be here next week—any of us."

"Right."

"Not only were they married in another life, they were also sister and brother in another life. They were great pals—all of this has been established over lifetimes. Your son admits that Peggy was supposed to move on. But he had a decision to make, and thought to himself, *Should I or shouldn't I?* But then when he realized she had crossed, then there was no question where he was going to go. And his decision wasn't to kick you in the pants or anything like that—it's just because they were soul mates in many different ways. He admits that he would have blamed himself had he stayed. He would have been haunted by the fact that she passed and he didn't. It would have been a tough cross to carry. It's not that he was a weakling, but he just wasn't ready to experience that lesson yet. Plus, he knew she'd need somebody to show her around over there."

(They laugh.)

"He has a good sense of humor. He's funny. I like his straightforwardness—he calls a spade a spade.

"So naturally the two of them are together and at peace, their part of the experience has been fulfilled, and they're very much around you like guardian angels. But they're also very glad, through their experience, to tell you what your life plan was in this life. He says you've been mother and children before—that life is one big wheel. He compliments you that you are fulfilling what you are supposed to do. It's not easy. You'd change your mind tomorrow if you could . . ."

"Yes."

". . . but then he says to me, *Or would you?* Because you're doing what you're supposed to be doing. And you're honoring them through what you are doing, as well as fulfilling your own individual journey. It's interesting—they also tell me you two have been together before. That's no surprise. And again, they're not saying this to be judgmental or insensitive, but they tell me their dad had to be out of the picture. He had to be there for the time he was, but then he had to be out of the picture. *(To Elaine)* They tell me you went a bit overtime in that relationship."

"Mmm-hmm."

". . . But your son states to me that so much of what we've been taught here is not how it has to be. He brings up a great example to me—for years, my own mother wouldn't go to Communion, because she married a divorced Protestant. Finally one day I said to her, 'Do you realize how much of that is horse manure?' It is—it doesn't change your faith. Things we've been taught about divorce being so taboo, your son says that seeing this attitude here sometimes pisses him off—because we seem so controlled. It's controlled through power, through fear, through guilt . . . things like that meant to keep you in line. But he says that's how the *club* survives. A smartass remark, but he does have a point. I wouldn't say your son was the religious type, but he was spiritual. He says, 'Where do people have the nerve here to tell others what God wants or what we should do?' He says the access to knowledge on the other side is infinity—it's endless. And so much of it can occupy his day over there because it's so fascinating. And when you really allow yourself, over there, to think and understand, it makes so much sense. But he says to give yourself credit because you are a survivor, and you are fulfilling your purpose here. Each day is one day closer. But the purpose is to go forward as you are, and to fulfill the plan."

"Okay."

"They bring up about pets that passed on, and I know that you've lost some. One of them was the actual pet of your children, yes? Because it's there with them. Your son likens his and Peggy's passing to a jar filled with puzzle pieces that gets smashed and the pieces go everywhere. And then it's your life's job to painfully put all those little pieces back together. They both thank you for understanding that one of them could not continue living without the other here. Even their passing together was part of their being soul mates. Even though Peggy passed, you thought for sure that Denis was going to pull through. And he didn't. Life is about choices, and he was given a rare opportunity—did he want to stay here, or go? Because of the purity of their relationship, he might have been put on the spot as to what he wanted to do. But even [if he had] continued here and they asked again, you know what his answer would be. But they're glad that you accept it, and that you see why it went the way it did. It makes so much sense—why were they together that night? The stage was set, and they went forward with the role. If it was supposed to go any other way, they would not have been together.

"Denis and his biological dad had a gap of communication at that time?"

"Yes."

"He is extending the olive branch from over there. That's his way of saying from his end he's settled the score. He does tell me that even for a while over there, he held on to a little bit of that resentment. But he says he had to learn for himself that it's like carrying an empty steamer trunk on your back—it serves no purpose and only weighs you down. Your son is pretty black and white."

"Yes."

"But what's funny is that over there, he had to learn to keep that pride in check. But for him, it was a tremendous sense of liberation. The pride, the resentment—he just learned to let it go. *(To Joe)* You certainly knew him before he passed?"

"Oh yes."

"He gives me the feeling that he likes you and he always did. Even if at times you might have wondered. *(They laugh)* Because he tells me you could be a bit of a ball breaker, too."

(Laughs) "You know it."

"He and you—two of a kind. But he says that to reach the top of that symbolic mountain over there, in order to come to complete harmony with yourself over there, you realize you need to cool down and listen. And you really come to understand it all. It's very liberating—and they say it makes you pure of heart. They show me the Beatitudes—*Blessed are the pure of heart, for they shall see God.* They find themselves and their harmony. They do also bring up their surviving sister. They know that sometimes a bereaved sibling doesn't know how to feel. She may not know what to make of this. But they're glad to see that she's basically gone on with her life.

Your kids do tell me that when they look back into this dimension, they are kind of glad to be out of here. There's so much trouble here. You should think of their passing in the sense that you have two children you know for a fact are in a safe and happy place. They live in a perfect world."

"Yes."

"There's talk of a white lace celebration around you, and it sounds as if they're talking about a birth—but not the kind of birth you think. The birth of a child seems symbolic, like the birth of a new career or a new direction. There's been talk between the two of you about moving?"

"Well, we're getting up there."

"Well, there's a great deal that attaches you to where you are. So for the time being, they encourage you to stay put. Nobody's getting younger, and the taxes aren't coming down, but there's so much there that's significant for you. Stay put for the time being. Your son says not to pull the alarm unless you have to. He says that things in the neighborhood are changing."

"Not really . . ."

". . . Not in the sense of the area going bad, but the fact that people you knew, neighbors, start dying off, things start changing, new faces—things change for you. But these are people who look out for you. You're blessed in that regard. That's why they say to stay put. Your son says you're still the glue that holds the house together. I know you're basically retired, but with regard to what you do, something new is coming your way. It's that symbolic birth they put in front of you. Something, even if it's for a limited time. And they joke that they don't know where you get the energy from."

(Joe) "I don't know where she gets it either."

"Well, the energy comes from the fact that you're fulfilling your experience here. You're fulfilling your purpose. It's your part of the bargain, so to speak. But you do enjoy it."

"I do."

"And that's a great lesson. They know you enjoy what you're doing, and there's great spiritual grace and benefit from it. They say you gain *sanctifying graces* in the hereafter. This could be the opportunity of a happy trip coming . . . where for once it's just the two of you and what you want to do. It's funny—it's almost as if somebody may offer it to you. Somebody may have a place in another state, or on an island or wherever. Out of hospitality they invite you to go over there. You might kind of hem and haw about it, but your kids encourage you to go."

"Okay."

"Okay, I'll be shocked if you say yes to this, but there's a Collette . . ."

"Yes!"

"Really? Okay. Holy Christmas, I almost told her to take a hike. Because she all of a sudden came into the room, and I got goose bumps and a very nice feeling from her. And started saying something about not having the most common name, but not to push her away. And she showed me Saint Collette and said, 'Just say it's Collette.' And she asked again not to push her away. And I'm thinking, okay. That's why I'm shocked you said yes to it."

"Her parents were with us for dinner just last week."

"Wow, okay. She passed kind of young. I'm glad I didn't push her away, and she's right, it's not a very common name."

"Yes."

"She calls out to her parents and people here."

"Wow."

"She also blesses you for being so . . . as she says, you don't realize your strength. She shows me the Rock of Gibraltar. You're not vain—you're not the type to pin a medal on yourself, but Collette says you don't realize you've been such a tremendous rock. She certainly calls to her parents and family, if you think they can deal with this . . ."

"Oh yes."

". . . she says you would not have expected her to show up today."

"Does she want me to tell them anything?"

"She says 'The best thing you can do is to tell them I embrace them with love.' And that she's all right. And happy. She says, and she doesn't mean it to sound cruel, but unfortunately her parents are a little out of it right now. I know bereaved parents can be a little flaky from such heartbreak. But the thing is that she embraces them with love. She keeps insisting that they understand she's all right and in a happy, safe place. So there must be a reason she feels the need to say that. It's not being said just because it sounds nice—there's purpose behind what she's saying."

"Okay."

"Hmm . . . I don't know what this means, but people come around you, Elaine, telling me they are your parents. Umm . . . your father says he made a mistake?"

"A big one."

"Oh, okay—you get it—that's all I need to know. He put a laundry basket in front of me, meaning that he wasn't going to air your laundry in public. He's that type of person. But he owns up to the fact that he made a huge mistake concerning you. One thing he'd never do in a million years—he admits he was wrong."

"Wow."

"The sad part about it? He says it took him to get to the hereafter to acknowledge it. And even there he didn't think he was wrong, and then finally came to realize he was wrong and there was no way around it. He apologizes for hurting your feelings. It's like . . . to be honest, it feels like he disowned you."

"He did."

"He seemed to come over by you, but he felt a little embarrassed. So he said, 'I abandoned her, I disowned her out of stupidity.'"

"He didn't believe in second marriages . . ."

"Okay, then I would agree with him that it was stupidity."

". . . and we had the blessings of the Church."

"He reminds me of what they call the Black Catholics—if the Church says it, that's the way it goes. No black or white."

"Yes."

"Your mom does come close and blesses you for being good to her while she was here. She doesn't mean to be insensitive, but she says your loss is her gain."

(She laughs.) "Yes. Wow."

"Okay, the souls tell me they have to go. Wow, talk about an abrupt exit. But I've held on to them too long, so I guess they have to go."

In a way, I was sorry to see them go. Sometimes the souls are like old friends who have been around forever. Some, like Denis and Peggy, have been.

I still think of Denis and Peggy as youngsters, even though it's clear they have grown up and matured. They see the world in a much bigger way, and there is something beautiful in how they talk about their being in the hereafter as a matter of fact, like it has always been that way, and *we* were the ones who needed to reckon with that. It was also interesting to me to see how Peggy and Denis wanted to move away from talking exclusively about themselves, and also help their mother understand that Denis's passage through a different door set Elaine on a journey through a different door as well. She is now a beacon in the lives of other bereaved parents, helping them to understand their loss and find hope.

There will always be a special place for Denis and Peggy in my heart, since they not only taught me a thing or two about life both here and hereafter, but also, in a beautiful way, created a reason for their parents to continue on the earth. No matter how many sessions I do, no matter how many reunions with the souls are had, it doesn't get any better than that.

Finally, I always say that however grim the circumstance or poignant the moment, something always comes along to bring you a smile, to allow you to find humanity and laughter. Once Elaine and Joe had said their heartfelt good-byes, Elaine turned to me and said, "I love the chairs!"

2

I'M GOING
TO STAY
WHERE
I AM ME

FLORIDA HIGHWAY PATROL TROOPER CHELSEA RICHARD

At this juncture in my life and career, I should not be at all surprised by the sheer ingenuity and resourcefulness of the souls when it comes to creating a way for someone to find peace and comfort when it is their time to walk from this existence to the next. But once in a while, a circumstance will arise in a session where we find out that the doors of our reality here and the doors of perception there, which are spinning in opposite directions, end up in perfect synchronization. This happens so that a soul who may have had reservations about moving through the door can come to a greater understanding of their purpose in this life and the next. Giving whatever assurances we need to make a peaceful transition between worlds seems to be an important job for the souls. But while I know the souls do whatever is in their power to make the transition as comfortable as possible, it's a rare occasion when a soul can come through and tell us clearly and poignantly about that experience and its meaning, as Chelsea Richard has managed to do.

I met Bruce and Linda Richard at a group session we hold every few months. Although these sessions are shorter than individual sessions, the experience, I believe, can be profound for everyone in attendance. People learn about the workings of the hereafter not only from their own loved ones but also from the souls visiting the other attendees of the session.

Something struck me about Bruce and Linda's session pretty early on. Their daughter, Chelsea, had come through and communicated about being hit by a car, asking them not to blame anyone, and saying that her passing was quick and painless. What was striking about Chelsea's message was her statement that she would not have been able to continue her life here *if* she had stayed.

I got hung up on the word *if.* I said to her in my mind, *Are you telling us you had a choice?* Since the session is not for me and the souls really don't care what I think, she continued on for the benefit of her parents and moved aside so that Linda's mother also had an opportunity to speak. Nevertheless, that *if* stuck in my mind.

It's rare that souls share this kind of insight into the machinations of the other side, so we invited the Richards back for a full session in order to learn what I believed would prove to be a significant lesson.

This is Bruce Richard's story, in his own words:

Chelsea was born May 10, 1983, at Spohn Hospital in Danville, Illinois. Shortly thereafter our family relocated to Patchogue, New York, where Chelsea had a pretty normal childhood until she was five years old, when Chelsea's mother and I divorced. This resulted in joint custody, which her mother and I shared. Her mother, Patricia; brother, Nicholas; and Chelsea lived with her maternal grandparents, Don and Jeanette, for a couple of years after the divorce. After her mother was able to move into her own home, Chelsea spent several years with her mother and had weekly visitations with me. During her formative years, Chelsea went to live with her maternal grandparents full-time. She went back to living with her mother during her last years of high school.

Chelsea seemed to be a very shy individual during her growing-up years. In middle school and high school, she did not have a large group of friends, unlike her brother, who was very popular. Chelsea wore glasses during her youth and that seemed to give her some anxiety. She was a very caring person and helped her relatives with babysitting in her spare time.

In high school, Chelsea did not attend any proms and did not have a steady boyfriend. After graduation, she attended Suffolk County Community College, where she earned her associate's degree in Criminal Justice. I have to admit that I attempted to convince her to pursue a different college major. Of course, like most children, she did not listen to my advice. Chelsea began working part-time as a code enforcement officer with the town of Brookhaven, Long Island. During this time, her maternal grandparents, who still greatly influenced Chelsea's life, moved to a retirement community in Ocala, Florida. It was their move that prompted Chelsea to start thinking about relocating to Florida.

One day in 2004, Chelsea called my wife, Linda, and I to tell us that she was going to apply to be a trooper with the Florida Highway Patrol. We were quite surprised because she had always been such an introvert; we never thought she would seriously consider being a police officer. She ultimately made several trips to Florida to complete the application process. Her journeys took her to northern Florida for parts of the process and to southern Florida for other parts. Chelsea embarked on this venture on her own and alone. I was shocked and proud that she did it . . . my little girl was growing up, and fast.

Chelsea was accepted into the Florida Highway Patrol and entered the FHP academy on June 20, 2005. I worried that she would not be able to tolerate the strict discipline and hard work involved in the academy because she had never experienced that type of training. Many of her fellow troopers were former military and had experienced similar treatment in basic training. Her brother, a former Marine, provided encouragement during her academy training. She graduated from the academy on January 12, 2006, and Linda and I attended the ceremony. I will always remember how she stood ramrod straight with the rest of the graduating troopers. You could see her pride and confidence.

On May 18, 2007, Chelsea married a fellow FHP trooper. They purchased a home and Chelsea began talking about having kids. Her husband, who was older than her, could no longer have children, so they decided to go with artificial insemination with donor sperm, which enabled Chelsea to become pregnant. Although the pregnancy appeared to be normal, Chelsea delivered her son on

July 9, 2009, three months premature and weighing only 1 pound 6 ounces. They named him Clayton Richard Valdes, and he would spend the next several months in the hospital because of his premature birth. It was a very trying time for Chelsea, but she did not let it get her down. She lived and breathed her son. Chelsea considered Clayton her little miracle, and she was so right. You would think that after what he had gone through during the beginning of his life, God would not have added to the challenge by taking his mother from him for the rest of his life.

Chelsea fought for Clayton on many issues. Because of his earlier health issues, she would rush him to the doctor or hospital for any illness, no matter how minor. She was criticized for doing this but that never stopped her, because she always felt she knew what was best for her son. Clayton did not develop his speech as quickly as other children, and Chelsea made sure he was admitted into special teaching programs to increase his learning and speaking ability. She saw that Clayton grew from a child who never spoke to one who would never stop talking. Clayton was her life, and I am sure she is his guardian angel and will always be there for him.

Chelsea's marriage did not stand the test of time, however. She and her husband divorced. The divorce was finalized only months before Chelsea's passing, although their separation was much longer. During this time, Chelsea fell in love with Jamie, another trooper. She had lunch with him only hours before the tragedy that took her life. They left the restaurant and kissed each other and professed their love for each other. He was set to propose to Chelsea on her birthday, exactly one week away from their last meeting.

It was a beautiful spring afternoon on May 3, 2014. I was in our backyard pulling up dandelions when I received the news about Chelsea. A seventeen-year-old girl and her friend were involved in a minor accident on Interstate 75. George Phillips, the father of the girl involved in the accident came to their aid and pulled onto the shoulder to make sure his daughter and her friend were not hurt. Chelsea was dispatched to the accident scene and was talking to the tow truck driver, John Duggan, who was there to take the car off the shoulder of the road. Then, a seven-car crash close to where they were standing caused a pickup truck to veer onto the shoulder, killing all three of them—Chelsea, George, and John. Chelsea and John died instantly at the scene, and George died in the hospital the next day. Chelsea's brother, Nick, had the terrible task of telling me that she had been killed. How hard that must have been.

Linda and I attended Chelsea's funeral in Ocala, Florida. I was amazed by the number of people whose lives Chelsea had touched. I heard nothing but praise for my daughter. Although the loss of her is overwhelming, the kind words I heard about how Chelsea lived her life were extremely uplifting. Her interaction with and help to others was very inspiring. I learned that Chelsea would help other troopers by altering their uniforms for them when needed. She would never hesitate to help out when possible. Chelsea was also known for being a jokester. I am told her sense of humor would light up a room. After Chelsea's death, I learned that the ringtone on her cell phone was the song "Brave" by Sara Bareilles. I have listened to that song many times since Chelsea's passing, and I can understand why it made such an impact on her. Chelsea was a shy little girl who grew up to be a trooper with the Florida Highway Patrol. It wasn't until she died that I learned just how brave she was.

THE SESSION

"Let's begin and see who comes to visit. Four people all come forward at once—a female, a male, and it seems to be . . . another male and female. Now, in that little group, without explaining anything, there is talk of the younger female, understood?"

"Yes."

"There definitely is talk of a daughter, and young by today's standards. (They acknowledge.) She says she is one of the first of the little group that came in. Also, without explaining—passed on not that long ago? Not like last week, but it's interesting that she still feels brand-new over there. And the only reason I'll go with it is that with no conception of time, even if she passed five years ago, it's going to seem to her that she just got there. She does speak of a sudden passing? It definitely comes out of left field, yes?"

"Yes."

"She showed me a ballpark—that would certainly mean out of left field to me. She just said to me, and I don't know how you feel about it, but it was purely accidental."

"Yes."

"Now this can be symbolic or mean exactly what I'm seeing. She did show me a uniform, which can symbolize two things: either she worked in or around them or it symbolizes work. I'll leave it with you and hope you understand what she's doing.

"I don't understand—she keeps giving me the impression she got clipped."

"Yes."

"Again I see the uniform, so there must be some connection. I'm just chuckling to myself because she just told me to be careful. I was brought up in the fifties and sixties, and she teased me that

I might have a little bit of a sexist mentality from the way we've been conditioned to think at that time. Obviously . . . she kidded me again . . . she wasn't a housewife. *(They nod.)* Must have had some kind of career, a professional one. As she states further—that in my time, it would have been like a 'good old boys' club.' So apparently what she means is a position that I would stereotype as for men only. One thing she does bring up is that she did break barriers, yes?"

"Yes."

"Career-wise. It's not that she was the only woman involved, but it's still men. Women would be the minority. That's what she meant when she said she broke barriers. In a world that could still be the 'good old boys' club.' Now in spite of the fact that she did pass young by today's standards, and it's a terrible tragedy, she still wants to make sure you know she had a fulfilling life up to that point. And that's all that's requested of us. She says it's the life in your years that count, not the years in your life. You might be inclined to feel she got cheated out of her life. She does bring a brother up, so I take it she has one . . ."

"Yes."

". . . who is here. *(They nod.)* Obviously close, yes? *(They nod.)* They seem to have a nice relationship. Not that *you're* not having terrible anxiety over this tragedy, but the reason why she singles him out is because sometimes the sibling who survives doesn't know how he or she is supposed to feel."

"Yes."

"She expresses congratulations to him. It feels like, whatever it is, it's already happened, so there may be something . . . in the not too distant past, that he may have achieved or 'elevated' with. It may be a matter of opinion, but she kind of did and didn't believe in a hereafter? (*They are unsure.*) She put up a fence in front of me, so that tells me she was on the fence about it."

"Good."

"She might be inclined to believe that you'll find out when you pass on. But right now, at the time, she would have been focused on her life, her career, and what's going on here, and not really worried about what's to come. She says that ultimately—no matter what anybody says—whether they believe in a hereafter or not—ultimately, we have to learn for ourselves. Just like in your unfortunate situation, only another set of bereaved parents can understand how you feel. She says it's an unfortunate learning of self. She also states she's come in dreams, yes?"

"Yes."

"She tells me this isn't the first time you're hearing from her. This is just another way, so there might have been other ways in the past. But she does report dream visitations. As long as the dreams are comforting visitations, then they're genuine. Anything that upsets you, don't pay attention to it. Also . . . oh, that's probably what she meant . . . again, and she's not trying to add salt to the wound, but she says she didn't know what hit her. (*They nod.*) There must have been some sort of vehicle business involved, because I keep feeling cars. And she states—initially, when she gets there, and she didn't know what hit her—to her, she's still alive. So she's thinking she's dreaming, or she thinks she survived. That's what she meant earlier when she said she 'survives' it. Yes, but not literally, in the physical sense. But she states that when she gets over there, first she thinks she's dreaming—which is something a lot of the souls have said because it's like one moment to the next.

Nobody announces over there what's happened. And she does talk about people being over there, welcoming her, who she did know were passed on. Which is why she said at first she thought she was dreaming. But . . . it's almost as though she was given an opportunity to go back or stay—and yet tells me . . . she wouldn't have been too keen on coming back.

"As much as you would prefer that, and she knows you would have taken care of her . . . she gives me the feeling she would have been like a vegetable. Because of the damage from the accident. But there was a brief period where she thought about whether to stay or come back. But, over there . . . she's fine and back to her old self. Coming back here, that would not have been the case. And she tells me that even though you might not have minded, she wouldn't have been comfortable being a burden to herself or anybody else, including her folks. She also gives me the impression that one of you feel you saw her—almost like out of the corner of your eye, you could have sworn she was there. And if it hasn't happened yet, it will, but don't go crazy looking for it. Just let it happen. But also just know that it's not your imagination.

On the other hand, she does kid with you that you feel sometimes you don't get enough signs from her, and yet you talk to her all the time. (They nod.) I don't mean to laugh . . . because she has a nice sense of humor . . . she says it's going right over your head. You feel her presence—your own intuition picks up on it, and it prompts you to speak to her. You don't have to be told who it is— you just know who it is. And she says you'll just speak to her. And she says then you'll think you're not getting a sign from her, and then there's one that goes right over your head.

"She just hopes you're not disappointed in her that she chose to stay. She wouldn't have been a happy camper if she came back.

She says to me, 'Who would want to live like that?' I'm not in your shoes, but I agree with her. And especially because, as she says, she knows because she had a brief vision of it from over there. She knows she would have been a burden to herself and whoever else. Also, as your daughter, she hopes you'll agree with her that you'd much rather know that she's okay and *herself* someplace else. She says you would have been heartbroken. She admits, had she stayed on the earth, she would have *been there and not there* . . . it would have been a very heartbreaking ordeal for you, as well as for *her*. It just doesn't look like it would have been the best of times. Whereas over there, she's all right and back to her old self. The only difference is that the physical body died. I don't mean to be insensitive, but she says someday you're also going to die, and somebody's not going to be too happy that *you* left, either."

"Yes."

"Okay . . . she shows me the uniform and talks about the 'good old boys' club.' She almost looks like she's a cop, but her uniform doesn't look like something I'm used to seeing around here. *(They nod.)* Okay . . . maybe she means state . . . that this happens out of state. Understood?"

"Yes."

"So . . . it's more affiliated with the state. In a police sense or something. *(They nod.)* Cute, too—maybe not the most patient gal in the world, because she says to me, 'Look, he gets it.'"

(They laugh.)

"She also wanted to bring up that even though she passed young, she still says she had a fulfilling life. Especially since she decided 'I'm going to stay where I'm me.' Because she also came to recognize that as much as you'd rather have her here, she's really *not* separated from you—only just by form. She says that even though she's closer to you than you can imagine, and that you've had evidences of that from her, she *can* say that as much as you miss her, she misses you—but only in the sense of *form*. And she says when your time comes, she'll be there to welcome you over. You'll have that to look forward to. But you're not going there anytime soon. *(They laugh.)* I like the cracks she makes. She cracks me up. She just hopes—as much as she knows it's not completely fulfilling compensation for you—as long as you know she's okay and in a happy place, hopefully you'll be able to sleep better tonight and this will be able to take some of the bite off.

She brings up that she knows you'll never be the same again—that's understandable—but she also compliments your perseverance. I don't know why, but as your daughter states, just don't ever think you did something wrong where this happened to you. Understood? *(They nod.)* She tells me to tell you that you think too much. That's why she doesn't want you to think you've done anything wrong, or screwed up somewhere where this is the result. It's nothing of the kind. She says that other souls say we cannot even *begin* to understand the cruel coincidences of this world on the earth. And she certainly is no holy roller, but she says the Divine Presence sends compensations if we look for them. You may think to yourself, *Who do I blame for this?* But there's nobody to blame. It just *happened*. She's your daughter, and she always will be—but she's also her own person, on her own unique experience here. That's the only thing that's different. And she fulfilled her experience here sooner than you. She knows you would gladly sacrifice your life for hers—'Thank you very much,' she says, 'but you're not supposed to be here yet.' But as she states, if anybody had told her she would pass on at this young age, she wouldn't have believed it. This is just not supposed to happen. She admits that when she first got over there, she was a little ruffled. She felt she wasn't supposed to be there yet. So, in a way, she may have wanted to 'complain to the management.' But that's when they told her to look at her life and what she had fulfilled, and if she wanted to go back, that's okay, but this is the way you're going to be. And she said her physical body was damaged. And then she came to realize that she was supposed to be over there.

She does thank you for praying for her in your own way. She also knows you don't know what the hell to believe anymore. But she kids you—you kind of do it for 'insurance purposes.' She shows me blocks falling into place—apparently her way of showing me that everything has fallen into place, even though at this time you may not understand. She says that the 'right way' we've been taught here isn't necessarily the right way they're taught over there. Interesting, though—since she's been there, she's kind of 'explored.' Obviously a very bright individual. Also she does thank you for the memorial, so apparently there are good things being done in her name and memory. Plus, she brings up many people who have done kindnesses on her behalf since she passed on. They may not have come up to you to tell you it has been done, but it doesn't mean she wouldn't receive the good intentions that come from it. One thing she does state is: she calls out in general to her family on the force. She speaks of a tremendous show up at her wake and funeral."

"Yes."

"She gets a very honorary acknowledgment. She received a hero's acknowledgment. She also realizes that her passing scared the you-know-what out of a lot of people. Especially in her career.

She brings up that she's glad to acknowledge—so she doesn't feel like her passing was in vain—it really taught a lot of her fellow officers to be *extra* careful while on duty. *(They nod.)* Especially if they pull somebody over. She's come to learn over there that there's a purpose behind everything. And she's pleased that it's made them look upon things and know they need to be a little more careful. Once again, though—and it must be important to her—she states that she had a fulfilling existence here, and she's come to recognize that."

"Yes."

"Again, she's telling me she got 'clipped,' and I'm thinking—without telling me—did she pull somebody over, were they too close to the road? But you know what she's doing. And not that she's being insensitive, but she says she wants to get past that. That's what happened, okay—but this is the way it is now. *(They nod.)* I'll tell you the truth—and I mean this with all love—your daughter is a nice gal. But she could be a tough nut to crack. *(They laugh.)* I wouldn't want to be pulled over by her. That's the thing—she's a sweetheart—but I can feel from her that she could be tough. But she says in many ways you have to be—you're holding up a principle. Like it says on all the police cars—'To Protect and Serve.' It's part of the job. Ohhh . . . that's what I was seeing. The name is Chelsea. Understood?"

"Yes."

"Now I can explain, and I'm glad I kept my mouth shut. Sometimes they come right out and say their name, and sometimes they show me something that I should pay attention to. But I kept seeing scenes from the movie *On Golden Pond*, and I kept asking myself what is she trying to tell me—what am I supposed to be seeing here? I just realized that the daughter's name in the movie is Chelsea. And she also showed me the Clintons, but I started thinking maybe she got some kind of presidential award, and I was taking it symbolically until I realized their daughter is also Chelsea. It's not a name you hear very much.

"She's obviously very close to her brother, yes?"

"Yes."

"She certainly calls out to him in love—whether he believes this or not. She tells me she's not here to make any converts. If he wants to believe it, wonderful—if not, he's going to come here and find out she was right as usual. (*They laugh.*) She's not too concerned—ultimately, because she's already been through it, she knows that you have to learn things for [yourself]. She says there are people going over there thinking that Saint Peter is going to meet them at pearly gates, and they've got it all figured out. But nobody says a word—they let them learn for themselves.

"She's giving me the high sign she's going to pull away, so I have to listen. She calls out in compassion to . . . somebody must have witnessed her getting clipped. (*They nod.*) They must have seen it. She says she's around like a guardian angel, but hopes you understand that she doesn't go around waving a magic wand. But hopes that as long as you know she is all right and in a safe, happy place—no complaints from over there—and you can tell she's glad she came to realize that even though she passed young, she did fulfill. Remember—the life in your years, not the other way around. But with that, she certainly embraces both of you with love."

In many ways, for me, this session was like having lightning strike twice. It's rare, but it happens. Similar to the Stillwells' son who made a choice to go with his sister, Chelsea was given a choice to stay or go, and she carefully weighed the options.

I think it has to be one of the most courageous things in the world for a soul to make the kind of a decision that Chelsea made. Knowing what they are leaving behind, not so certain of what they are walking into ahead. It's easy to know after the fact that they are happy with their decision—who wouldn't be, surrounded by love, peace, and joy in the hereafter? But think about that moment—the moment in which the decision must be made. Here you stand— with everything you know and love in one hand, and in the other hand, the lure of peace, lightness, and joy. Chelsea chose well. The souls know that someone can be a better mother, daughter, sis-ter, friend, and colleague in the hereafter than they could ever be on the earth; in the hereafter, they have the capacity to live in the hearts of those who know and love them. It's that moment of choosing that is so brave. For Chelsea, the true measure of her soul was revealed in that moment.

In honor of Highway Patrol Trooper Chelsea Richard, Gover-nor Rick Scott vetoed a bill that would have increased the speed limit on some Florida roadways to 75 miles per hour. Florida has enacted and enforces a "Move Over Law" and in Chelsea's honor, designated the month of June to be "Move Over–Slow Down– Save a Life" month. It is their hope that a tragedy like this one will never happen again. Chelsea's son, Clayton, is growing and thriv-ing with his father, and often attends the memorial services and ceremonies that honor his mom.

3

A GOOD ACTOR

EVAN NASKY

*Dear Angel, tell this to my mother, Tell her
    that I will always love her.
Tell her that she always means so much to
    me. Tell her that when there,
I wouldn't be afraid of a grizzly bear. Tell
    her that she always knew,
That I always loved you know who. Now be
    off with you!
Fly to the sky that's a deep blue.*

—Written by Evan Nasky in fourth grade

The Nasky family appeared to be every bit the ideal American family—people who actually like one another, people who conduct lovely, contented, well-lived lives. Attractive and well dressed, the husband, wife, and daughter came into the conference room and took their seats with casual confidence. Brian, the father, gave me a broad smile as he shook my hand. I actually expected this to be an in-and-out session, the kind I have done dozens of times for well-meaning people who have lost their grandparents at a ripe old age, or just have a general curiosity about mediumship. But looks can be terribly deceiving. I was not prepared for what came through as this lovely family sat down. As I began the session a young man appeared, pacing, giving me the feeling he didn't know quite how to begin without unleashing a tsunami of regret and sadness. More on this later.

This is the story of Evan, in his family's own words:

In 1991, in the spring of the year Evan was born, we moved to Oahu, Hawaii. As a family, we spent a lot of time at the beach. From the time Evan could crawl, he loved to get into the water. As soon as he was mobile, he headed for the surf. He would crawl into the water and get knocked back by the waves. But Evan was an absolutely fearless toddler. He would get back up after being knocked over by the waves and crawl right out into the surf again. Evan's determination was absolutely amazing, and this remained true during his entire life.

When Evan was three years old, we moved to Austin, Texas. He wasn't used to wearing shoes at all, and we had a difficult time acclimating to the terrain of Texas. For several months after the move, Evan often asked me, "Mommy, where the ocean?" It was hard to explain to a three-year-old that the ocean he loved was very far away. Once we settled in the Austin area, I enrolled Evan in a local day school. There he met one of his best friends, Sean. The boys remained close friends all during elementary school and middle school, and then Sean moved when Evan was in high school. The boys kept in touch on the computer through video games in later years. Evan always visited Sean when he was home on break once he was in college. After Evan died, he appeared to Sean and several other friends in dreams that let them know in no uncertain terms that there was indeed life after life, and that he still loved them very much.

Evan was in the gifted and talented program at his elementary school from the time he was in first grade. He took his work very seriously and did many in-depth projects. He was an inquisitive, bright, talented student all throughout elementary school and into middle school. But, more than that, he was sweet.

During his middle school years, Evan became interested in choir. I found out that Evan had a wonderful singing voice at one of his early middle school performances, when he sang and danced to "Putting on the Ritz." I'll never forget that performance. I think it may have been the start of Evan's theatrical "career." Evan was cast in the middle school production of *Footloose* later in his eighth-grade year, and from that performance on, there was no stopping him.

Once in high school, Evan was totally serious about his studies in theater. To him it was already a profession. He was cast in every production during his four years of high school and from sophomore year on won principal roles. Evan won many awards during his high school years in theater and had the lead in a one-act play for the state finals competition in his senior year. To Evan, his fellow theater students were extended family.

Evan was recruited by many universities. Though he had numerous scholarship offers, he chose to attend the University of Evansville in Indiana, because of his love of theater. Evan had a focus and determination throughout his college years that was nothing short of amazing! We knew that he was struggling in some areas, though none of them were academic. When he was never given any stage roles at UE, the disappointment began to take a toll on him, and we could see a difference in his behavior when he returned home. We talked about it. His response was that theater was like a marathon: you had to be prepared to be in it for the long run.

In the early hours of the morning of March 3, 2012, a terrible tragedy befell our family. Our beautiful, beloved son and brother, Evan Nathaniel Nasky, died by suicide. He had recently turned twenty-one and was in the second semester of his junior year. Spring break was beginning, and Evan was preparing to act in one production and direct another scene in the coming weeks. We had spoken to Evan by phone the Thursday before he died and planned on being there for his performance the following weekend.

While we know that his transition was felt keenly by his friends, the UE Theater Department has never contacted us, other than sending a representative to his memorial service. There was a huge showing at his memorial service, with both teachers and friends who truly cared about Evan.

So many people reached out when they heard of Evan's loss to the disease of depression, which led to his suicide. His death was a total shock to both family and friends. None of us saw or realized what was happening to him. He was too talented, too intelligent, too logical, too funny, too sincere, and too open to be suffering from a disease unbeknownst to us all! We had talked to him two days before and we could tell his voice was different, but we did not see the reality; we saw a son who was tired and in need of a spring break. No amount of pain or desire can give another chance at that phone call. This tragedy will haunt us forever.

Not until we subpoenaed records from the university did we discover that Evan had been in counseling, and that he had mentioned having suicidal thoughts. It is true that Evan did seek help, but the level of help available was not enough, and it was not effective. If we had known that Evan had been having suicidal thoughts, we would have moved heaven and earth to help him.

Evan and I had a discussion one day as we drove home through a spring thunderstorm near the end of his sophomore year in high school. By that time, Evan had developed an investigative and scientific mind. He was interested in spiritual matters, but had a healthy skepticism regarding the teachings of organized religion. We were discussing a dream that I had had about my dad thirty days before he died of Parkinson's disease, when Evan was in middle school. In the dream, my dad appeared to me as I remembered him from my childhood. He was young, strong, and healthy. He explained to me that he was getting ready to move to his new house and wanted to show it to me. He took me inside a building and began to open door after door into spectacularly beautiful places filled with incredible beauty. Evan listened thoughtfully, as always, and then explained to me that he felt this was my subconscious mind attempting to comfort me, rather than an actual visitation from my dad. He was very sweet and kind about his explanation. I loved to discuss spiritual matters with him, because he always allowed for my feelings and opinions, even while he did not have the same beliefs. After we got home that evening he drew a diagram of several theories, including string theory, that might account for other realities after death.

One summer evening, the creek below our house was aglow with fireflies. There were so many that at first I thought there was someone out there with a flashlight. I asked Evan to go investigate with me. We went for a walk down into the woods below our house and I jokingly told him that the fireflies were "fairies" from the spirit world, and that we were in a magical "wonderland." As usual, Evan humored me, and then proceeded to explain the science behind the glow of the firefly. It was rather amazing to me that he knew this, since I had no idea what actually made the fireflies glow. He was so kind, so sweet, so gentle. Being with him there in the woods surrounded by fairies in a magical wonderland is a memory I will hold dear in my heart forever. When the fireflies come out each year, I feel that part of Evan is here with us. There is nothing but sweet memories of the boy who was—and is—the light of our lives. We could write a book of thousands of pages about his life. We have thousands of photos of him. We will never give up on his life, which we know goes on. We are sure that Evan is exploring his new home with the same imaginative curiosity that he had here on earth. We love you, son and brother, now and forever! You are the best son anyone could ever have!

THE SESSION

"Okay, so let's begin. Immediately a male presence comes forward . . . he actually came in with you . . . and with him are two females. Okay, a male came forward, so I take it you understand."

"Yes."

"He's saying he's the son, he's the brother. (*They nod.*) You're his family—you're his immediate family."

"Yes."

"First thing he states—and there must be real purpose behind this—he does state that he is all right and in a happy place . . ."

"Okay."

". . . and it seems very . . . as a family in your sad circumstances,

I'm sure you want to hear that, but there seems to be more purpose behind it."

"Yes."

"He's not just saying it because it's a nice thing to say—there seems to be a real reason behind it. He does speak of grandparents being with him. Just so you know that he's not alone. He certainly does speak of a tragic passing, yes?"

"Yes."

"Age, of course, but circumstance also."

"Yes."

"Funny, he said he knew he was going to pass on. Huh. I don't think he made a public announcement, but . . . hmm, I have to be careful with this—he did speak of an accidental passing, yes?"

"Uh, no . . ."

"I knew you were going to say no, but I think I know what he may be drifting toward. That's why . . . I can explain it later. He doesn't die in a car accident."

"No."

"But it does seem to be a sudden passing. He shows me a ballpark—which means it comes out of left field. He does speak of having had health trouble, but more so in the emotional sense?"

"Yes."

"He does bring up about a lot of times not being the happiest person here, understood?"

"Yes."

"Because . . . yeah, he admits he does suffer in silence, yes?"

"Mmm-hmm."

"He does admit—kind of a good actor?"

"Mmm-hmm."

"He just gives me the impression that if I knew him when he was here, I, too, would have been shocked by his passing . . . and again, insists that you know he's all right and in a happy place. That's not going to cure anything, but he hopes it will take the bite off. Also—I heard the name Brian called, understood?"

"Yes."

"Also, too—unless you didn't think so—toward the end, your son was being a little distant?"

"Yes."

"Not that he wasn't speaking to you. But it's a feeling like he's there and he's not there. Toward the end of his life. *(They nod.)* Very sensitive guy. Fantastic trait, but also trouble. He talked about passing in a sleeplike state."

"Yes."

"A very complex individual. Not meant in the negative sense. He gives me the impression [of]—at the time of his passing—not being in the right frame of mind."

"Yes."

"I was pretty positive I was in the right thought pattern, but it's up to the soul to say it. He kind of apologizes that he deceived you. Like—you thought everything was okay, but it wasn't. Good actor, again. He definitely had gone through significant struggle, understood?"

"Yes."

"Not that he did it intentionally, but he does feel he kind of deceived you. Earlier he had given me the impression that he had contributed to ending his own life. That's why he said 'accident.' Because I don't like the S-word. I've learned from over there that there's a lot more going on . . . somebody just doesn't wake up one day and decide, 'I'm going to take my own life.' There has to be . . . there's a health problem. That's why I know at first when I said 'accident,' you said no, but he said to me, 'You know where I'm gonna go,' and I thought, *Yup. But I'll just let you take your time.* And that's why it comes up as an accident—because at the time of his passing he's not in the right frame of mind, and he can't be held responsible for his actions. Also—unless he just felt like everything was piling up on him—he was having trouble with career?"

"Yes."

"He talks about having trouble with 'career,' and tells me to say to you all, 'This was not the smartest thing to do.' But he's not in the right frame of mind. He does express to me, and I'm sure you understand, too, that he wishes he had given himself more time. But it's almost like, to a degree, he had a breakdown and he didn't know it. He wants to make sure none of you feel that you failed him in any way. Like you should have known something was up. He's not a big crybaby, he's not whining about everything. In his case, he shows me a time bomb. He shows me a volcano—things are simmering and building up. Sadly, he shows me a snowball, going down the hill and getting bigger and bigger. This certainly is not a stupid person. It's obvious that he's bright. He has friends; everybody likes him and loves him. And yet on the other hand, we have to try and understand that he doesn't know what triggered it. One thing he does admit, he was kind of hard on himself, understood?"

"Yes."

"Yes and no, understood? Because every time he says something like that, he pulls me back. He gives me the impression he might not have let you know what was going on in there. He put a dark curtain in front of all of you—you might have been kept in the dark to a good degree. You *know* him—but that's the Dr. Jekyll part, and there's a part of him you do and you don't know. It seems you're a very close family, so there's no problem there . . . he gives me the impression everything was going downhill, but it wasn't. Strange as this is going to sound, he's also kind of a lonely guy—and yet has people who love him and like him. And yet at times, even if he didn't share it with you, he tells me he doesn't believe he's really liked. I'm not trying to be funny but he shows me the scene in the *Wizard of Oz* where the wizard says, 'You're the victim of disorganized thinking.' And that's what was happening to him—he became the victim of his own disorganized thinking. But he did have a letdown in a relationship, yes? (*They nod.*) Because he definitely felt he got dumped. Not that he's blaming anybody, but that is a contributing factor—he's not going to BS me. He gave me the impression—without saying anything—he was married, or thought he was going in that direction. It seems to be . . . was the relationship pretty steady?"

"We don't know."

"Oh, okay. It's kind of like he sets everything up in his mind—in the sense of like, he's going to achieve *this*, and *this*, you know? (*They nod.*) But then when it doesn't fall into place, he falls apart. Again—he's an *achiever*. I'm not in your shoes, but I can't believe what I'm hearing from him. Yes, indeed, he's an achiever, but he says that too much achievement is as bad as too little.

"Again, that feeling he gives me—I see an orderly file cabinet— he's always been very orderly. Things, as he states, were not lining up the way he had anticipated. Or the way he thought they should."

"Yes."

"And it's sad to hear him say from over there that he should have given himself more time. Because he's seen that, okay, something may not have happened on a specific date, but it would come to pass later on. As he's come to learn over there, you can't put yourself on a rigid schedule. You can't say, 'This is going to happen on this date.'"

"Yes."

"And that's why he's so glad that the Divine Presence has given him the opportunity to reach out, because this has left you all hanging. He recognizes that he was successful. But then he says to me that success is very difficult to deal with. You can pressure yourself into thinking you have to maintain it all the time. He must not have really shown that he could be depressed. *(They nod.)* It's there, but he shows me a blanket—he is good at covering it. This doesn't mean that he's in any state of unhappiness, so don't read between the lines, but he's kind of angry with himself . . . that he did this. Because he knows there was no reason to. Not that there's ever a reason. But he states that it's almost that he didn't know how to let himself *feel* that way, understood?"

"Mmm-hmm."

"But he wasn't in the right frame of mind. *(They nod.)* He's not thinking. That's why I have to agree with him that this is an 'accidental' passing—like passing from an illness in the emotional sense.

"And the strangest thing is that now, over there—it's almost like . . . again, he admits it wasn't the brightest thing to do, and he wasn't in the right frame of mind—my heart goes out to him. But even *now* he's confused, like, 'Why the hell did I do this?' And this feeling of *what happened??* And the thing is, he snaps his fingers at me, like this is *(snaps his fingers)* an abrupt, out-of-nowhere thing. I wish you could be in my brain for ten minutes, because you'd hear this part of the brain listening and absorbing what he's saying, but the other side saying, *I don't believe you,* I can't believe you let this happen. He states, and he sure is right—this session, nothing is going to cure your grief. *(They nod.)* That's why he just hopes [that] what he can address or explain—maybe it will take the bite off.

"He also states he has come in dreams. He insists this is not the first time you are hearing from him. You have heard from him. *(They are unsure.)* Also—you might feel as though you've seen him. Like from the corner of your eye, you'd swear he was there."

"Yes."

"There was like, a falling in his passing?"

"Yes."

"I don't know what he means, and I want to keep my mouth shut for now. But I feel like I'm falling. It does contribute to his passing—that's what he states."

"Yes."

"He speaks of an injury to the head—not like somebody bashed him on the head, but internally. *(They nod.)* I feel the oxygen cut off to the heart and brain. *(They nod.)* It feels like an injury. I hope this doesn't add salt to your wounds, but he said to himself, *What was I thinking?* But that's why we have to be completely compassionate to the sense that he was not in the right frame of mind. Now that he's there, and okay, clear-headed and knows what's happening, I can really understand him saying, 'What the hell was I thinking?' Because if you're not in a rational state of mind, you don't know any better.

"If he was on the earth and I put him on the spot and talked about a hereafter, he'd be inclined to say, 'When you're dead, you're dead.' He would have leaned toward that. And this is what is heart-breaking for him over there. He figured you're dead and that's the end of it—you go into nothingness. But he's realized that no, there is something, and he can feel your reactions here. And he feels a dreadful sense of helplessness that he can't do anything about it."

"Yes."

"A lot of times things are never good enough for him. Also—he did thank you for the memorial. *(They nod.)* A lot of good things being done in his memory. I'm sure not just by all of you, but also people he knew. He talks about many people doing kindnesses on his behalf since he passed on. And even though he says he's closer to you than you can imagine, and you've had evidence he's near, he knows it's not the same thing. So again—he's reached out, where you feel you've seen him, he's come in dreams . . . he's *trying* to give evidences to let you know he's near, and that he's all right. And to his sister, he does reach out—obviously you and he were very close. And [he] knows you're heartbroken—you wonder why, if something was bothering him, why didn't he talk to you?"

"Mmm-hmm."

"He felt a little shy about talking to his folks . . . he realizes now he shouldn't have been, but there's a part of him that didn't want you to see his weaknesses. He speaks of his grandmothers being with him . . ."

"Yes."

"Mom, your mother reaches out to you to say that she's with him, because you've prayed to her to look out for him."

"Yes."

"She says that she's seen your tears and heard your prayers. She says, 'So know he's with me.' It's not going to cure anything, but they hope it will make things easier if you know. So they are both there with him, and your mom states that as the dad, you suffer very much in silence, so this is a very personal thing between you and her. I do see Saint Patrick appear. It could mean Irish heritage, or a blessed positive symbol. So if the name Patrick doesn't mean anything to you, and I don't feel that's the case, then take it as a very positive symbol. And he does talk about a tremendous show up at his wake and funeral."

"Yes."

"I see people coming out of the woodwork. He sees how much he was loved and liked. People must have been completely horrified by the news. *(They nod.)* Seeing this, every now and then I myself feel like I can't even speak—I'm completely dumfounded by what happened here. Unless I'm misunderstanding—he hasn't been there very long?"

"No."

"He's definitely very close to you this time of year. Christmas is a very sentimental time, and it's a tough obstacle to get through. He knows that sometimes you wish you could just fall asleep and wake up after the New Year. *(They nod.)* When most families look forward to this time of year, you don't."

"Yes."

"Once again, you've heard it already, but he apologizes for his passing. This was not the smartest thing to do. He did *not* expect there to be anything afterwards, after this life."

"Yes."

"This is the thing that's driving me crazy: yes, not being in the right frame of mind, but why didn't he give himself that extra ten minutes? I feel swollen in the throat, like he hung himself."

"Yes."

"He just hopes that if you know he is all right, it will take some of the bite off. He also hopes you're not mad at him. Because he's frustrated with himself. He did thank you for the planting."

"Yes."

"I didn't say this before—earlier when he thanked you for the memorial, I saw a tree shoot up in front of you. So either a tree was planted, or something took root in his remembrance. Your dad passed, too, yes?"

"Yes."

"It's funny—when your son first got there, he thought he was dreaming. He says that you think you're almost . . . between the two dimensions, just thinking you're going to fade out, and then you find out it doesn't happen. He goes back to his school days when you were taught that energy can neither be created nor destroyed. But I think with this, he's going to pull back. Certainly a very emotional time for all of you, but also a release for him. To get a lot off his chest. And he hopes that it helps you a little bit as well. Whatever you think about life after death, he's the proof that he got caught with his pants down. He's not a fan of organized religion by any means, but he says you have to separate one from the other—religion and spiritual belief. But that's the problem with people believing in a hereafter—people usually associate that with organized religion. He does tell me there is no deity over there— there's no bearded presence. There's a Divine Presence. It's love and light. It's been an eye-opener for him, too. And he's certainly taken some time to explore and learn over there. But with this he tells me he's going to pull back—he embraces all of you with love. He knows this isn't a cure-all, but he embraces you all with love and hopes that as long as you know he's all right and in a happy, safe place . . . he admits, though, that it does frustrate him because he knows you'll never be the same again. You certainly want to know he's all right and in a happy place, and he reaches out to the three of you. And . . . I don't mean to laugh, but your son has a sense of humor, and he says, 'You can even pray for me.' *(They laugh.)* Because that would be so out of left field for him. He's not telling you to say formal prayers, but any prayer embraces him with love. It comes to the souls like gifts. But with that, he pulls back, and the others do, too . . . and there they go."

This session was unusually unsettling for me. There had to be more to this. I had never had a soul just come out with the unvarnished truth and say, *What the hell have I done?* This was very unusual, and not the standard protocol of any session I'd ever had in the past. Most of the souls who take their own lives try to softpedal some of the details to spare their family any more agony, but this young man seemed hell-bent on explaining that even *he* doesn't know what he was thinking. I couldn't help feeling sorry for this boy, although I shouldn't—at the end of the day, he's getting better care than we can imagine. But it doesn't stop the agony of thinking *why?* I knew this session was going to be a blow to the family; I wondered if the whole thing was going to do more harm than good. I thought, *You can't just show up, tell us you ended your life and you don't even know why, and then say, "Bye, folks, it's been fun."* The session ran very long that day, I remember—and still it didn't feel like Evan was finished speaking. It almost felt like he wanted to go on forever. It was clear he hated what he had done to his beautiful family. And my heart ached for him. I got the feeling he wasn't completely finished. Nothing got settled, nothing got fixed.

Shortly after the session, I called Andrew, my coauthor and program director, to talk about this lack of resolution. I was so disappointed that this boy had spent so much time trying to make sense of something truly senseless, something even *he* didn't completely understand. I could feel it in my bones that Evan wanted another shot at making things right.

Andrew told me we had received an email from Brian Nasky, in which he politely expressed some concerns about the session. He wrote that although the session had connected them with their son, the family felt no sense of relief. Hearing Evan try in so many ways to apologize for what he had done had actually made things worse for them. Andrew and I told Brian it was pretty clear that Evan was not finished talking, and we predicted that he needed more time to help them find resolution in all of this.

Andrew arranged for a second session to be held via telephone so that I would not recognize them or the number I was calling. It was up to Evan to start fresh. As we expected, the second session was vastly different from the first. This time, unburdened of the need to justify his actions, Evan moved on to telling us about his new world, about what he had learned and what he was continuing to learn about himself. It was a marked improvement over the pall of the first session—we communicated with a boy at peace with himself. The family, thankfully, felt the session was healing.

It was interesting to note that Brian Nasky's email after the first session made it clear that they were looking for the kind of comfort and feeling of peace that can be the end result of a session. What the Naskys had not counted on was that the unvarnished truth is much more powerful, and their son was determined to give them clarity at all costs. He felt he owed that to them.

The souls know better than I that it's never too late to have a happy ending—even if they sometimes need to push us into allowing them to speak enough times to help us understand this. They know what to do and when, regardless of our expectations. This is why we must trust them with the task of leading us down the path of comfort, hope, and, eventually, acceptance.

4

THE GOOD SAMARITAN

JOSEPH BIDOT

In my line of work, sometimes I find the souls, but most of the time, they find me. I would have never known about Joseph Bidot had it not been for his cousin Anthony Bidot, who is in law enforcement on Long Island, New York, and who has been a good friend of mine for some time. Joseph, nineteen, was killed in a head-on collision, and there seemed to be no clear reason for his car to have veered into oncoming traffic. Neither the coroner, the state police, nor his family had any real idea what caused the accident.

This story not only touched me emotionally but also piqued my interest as a medium in a very significant way. Anthony told me about a man, a stranger, staying with Joseph at the crash site until he passed, a detail that started the whirring sound in my head that lets me know the souls are preparing to communicate. A funny thing started to happen when Anthony told me the story: I began to see backward through many of this boy's lifetimes on the earth, all the way through to the biblical account of the Good Samaritan.

The Good Samaritan is a parable told by Jesus and recounted in the Gospel of Luke. The parable relates the story of a Jewish journeyman who is robbed of his belongings, stripped, beaten, and left for dead by thieves. As he lay in the road, he is passed first by a priest and then by a Levite. The man is finally helped by a Samaritan, who stopped to help even though Samaritans and Jews were enemies at the time.

It struck me that there was much more to the way Joseph Bidot passed than a simple random act of kindness performed by a stranger. This contemporary reenactment felt more like a connection made to that incident long, long ago.

I wanted very much to meet somebody from the family of this young man, so the blanks in what seemed to be an incredible story could be filled in. The souls told me there was both an amazing story and a real learning opportunity for me here, so I reached out to the family. Did they have any interest in hearing from their son? Joseph's mother, Cary, said yes. She couldn't believe her luck. I couldn't believe mine.

This is Cary's story, in her own words:

My son Joseph was born on June 25, 1991. He was a child who loved people. When he was young he was a storyteller—he would tell us a lot of stories of having lived in another life. He always referred to a time when he was bigger, in another life, as opposed to seeing himself as a child. He would try to put Lego blocks together, and he would get frustrated. Instead of saying something like, "I'm mad because I can't do this," he would say, "When I was bigger, I could do this." Once we saw a blue Ford pickup, and he told us that was the truck he had before he died in a boat accident. On another occasion, we were visiting the site in a housing development where my sister was having a house built, and at only four years old, Joseph said, "I know this place—I drove a bulldozer right over there." He would say many unusual things that referred to a life or lives before this one, and we generally chalked it up to a vivid imagination.

Joseph hated school early on. He was dyslexic and had dysgraphia, which is an impairment of the ability to write. It made things really hard for him in school. His kindergarten teacher was wonderful with him, but other teachers were very tough on him. Some didn't seem capable of dealing with kids who had reading or writing problems. I think the constant frustration really was a negative influence on him, and I think this damaged his wanting to learn early on. Where we were very easygoing and unstructured at home, school seemed very demanding. Some of the teachers blamed his learning problems on me, telling me I treated Joseph too much like a baby. I should have pulled him out of that school, but that was a mistake I made, trusting their judgment. They may have made him feel bad about learning, but they couldn't dampen his spirit.

Joe was a precocious child. One day I was taking my older son to Boy Scout camp with Joseph in tow. While we were at the cabin dropping off my son's things, Joe ran ahead of me. I ran after him and found him a little ways ahead, talking to a stranger. I grabbed him when I caught up with him and told him, "Joe, you don't talk to strangers!" And he looked at me and said, "He's not a stranger."

And when I told him, "Joe, a stranger is a person you don't know," he looked at me with a confused look on his face and said, "But I know everybody! I don't know any strangers, only friends I haven't met yet!" That's the way he was as a child—happy, and so independent. One day, both my older children were playing soccer on two different fields on the playground. I was standing between the two fields, watching Joe play on the playground equipment there. I turned my head, and a second later, he was gone. I was alarmed and called out for him, and the play on the fields came to a stop while other parents came out to help look for him. A few minutes later, I found him in the parking lot. I asked him why he had wandered away, and he told me he thought I was at the car. He didn't see me because some people had blocked his sight of me on the field, so being as independent as he was, he just decided to walk to the car to wait for me there. That was how his mind worked all the time.

How can I explain Mr. Joe to people who don't know him? He was a clown, he loved to make people laugh, and he loved to make me laugh and shock me. He loved cars, and he dreamed of being a drift racer when he got older. And he *loved* the girls.

During junior high school, Joe started having incidents where he would black out. He would be fine one second, and the next would fall over and faint. We brought him to the doctor, and one by one the doctors all told us that Joe was just dehydrated and needed water. Every time, we were told it wasn't a heart problem. Once, when he said he was having chest pains, we brought him to the hospital. They did an EKG, but it appeared normal, and once again we were told he could just be dehydrated. Joe started going everywhere with a bottle of water, and started getting sick of having to constantly drink the water, telling me once after yet another dehydration diagnosis, "Mom, how much water can I drink?" He would carry a gallon jug of water with him everywhere. And when he couldn't get water, he would panic, because he associated lack of water with passing out.

While Joe was in college, we had a policy that education was more important than holding down a job. In addition to the money we gave him, he would earn a little here and there by doing odd jobs: fixing people's cars, doing car detailing, and, although he didn't get paid for this, helping people with their landscaping and mowing lawns, just because he was a good guy. His friends knew they could count on him at any hour of the day or night if they got stuck. Joe saved all his money to buy his first car, and we helped a bit, so he could buy his baby—a used Honda that had actually belonged to his older brother. My husband would take my sons to the auto auctions, buy a car at a good price, and the boys would fix them up. Joe was just like my husband in that he was excellent with cars, even though they didn't have much else in common. So Joe fixed up another car that he eventually traded with his brother for his baby, the Honda. He really loved that car—he drove it all the time and was so proud of it.

Joe used to love to shock me, or say things he knew would get a rise out of me. He was a big jokester that way. He used to say, "Mom, I know I'm going to die in a car accident, but not until I'm forty." And I used to say, "Shhh—don't say that to your mother!" But as much as he liked to shock me, he was also a kindhearted kid. About a week before the accident, he came to see me at work, which is part of the same college he was attending. He came into the office and said to me, "Mom, I just want to thank you for always understanding about my girlfriend. I'm just glad I can always talk to you, and I just want to thank you." He was about two weeks away from graduating from the school with his certification in welding, and he was looking forward to being able to work on cars and make a living.

On Wednesday, June 1, 2011, I was having a stressful day at work. We had just changed over to a new computer system, and I was working overtime trying to bring it up to speed. I had had to work the entire weekend before; that Monday was a holiday, but I worked that day, too, so I didn't get to see Joe over the weekend. He did stop by my office that day, but I didn't see him because I was in a meeting. A little later on, I took a break from work to meet some people from church for dinner. While I was talking to one of the church members, I was about to say something about wanting Joe to get back into the church, but something in my head yelled at me and said, *Say something nice*—and it startled me so much that I couldn't even think of what to say after that. After dinner I went back to the office to finish some work.

Joe was at his cousin's house, helping to pull a transmission out of a car. He started not feeling well, so he told his cousin he was going to go home, which was only about four miles from our house. He got in his car and started heading home down Yelm Highway. We don't know why, but somehow he drifted over the center line. His car and a car driving in the opposite direction, who apparently did not see him coming and didn't swerve, collided head-on. Joe died at the scene just a few minutes later.

The story made the local news because my older son is a state trooper. I knew I had to get in touch with my daughter before she saw it on the news. But while I was talking to her, she received a

Facebook message about her brother passing away. It was all over the place. My nephew and niece, whose parents also work for the state patrol, knew, but told their children not to post it to any social media. But you know teenagers—they don't understand the concept of waiting on something like this.

One benefit of the story having gone to all the media is that there was a story in the *Daily Olympian* online about Joseph, including a comments section. There were people speculating that he was speeding, or that there were drugs or alcohol involved—none of which was true. Some of his friends left comments about him, and so did his girlfriend, who wrote a long post. His girlfriend got a message from a man named Jason asking if she was his wife, and she explained she was his girlfriend. Jason replied that he was at the accident and was there with Joe before he died. He provided his phone number, and I called him. He asked if he could meet us, and of course we wanted to meet him. He came over to the house, and I had so many questions a mother would want to know about her son and the way he passed.

Jason came upon the accident almost immediately after it happened. He walked over to the car and saw that Joesph was alive but in shock. He told us Joe didn't look like he was aware that he had been in an accident, and that Joe was aware that he, Jason, was there, but didn't say anything. Joe was pinned behind the wheel. Jason told us that he took Joe's hand and recited the Lord's Prayer until Joe passed away. He stayed with Joe until the paramedics came and took Joe away. I don't know if anybody could even understand what Jason did for a mother that day. And for Joe. To know that my child did not die alone that day is so important to me.

It was a hard time for us. I'm dealing with things the best I can;

it's still hard, though. People always say that it gets better. It's not that it gets better; you just learn how to deal with it better. My grief is still there—my grief will always be there, because I want my son back. But as time goes on, I realize he's not coming back. For the first month I sat by the front door, expecting him to walk through the door, saying, "Joke, Mom!" Even after I saw his body, I still couldn't process the fact that he was gone. His cause of death was internal bleeding as a result of the impact, but after the autopsy we found out that he did have a heart issue after all. They found that his body was deteriorating because his heart wasn't pumping blood properly, and he wasn't getting enough oxygen to the brain. He may have blacked out behind the wheel, but they could not say so with any certainty. You just don't think that a nineteen-year-old would have any heart issues, but I still believe that for reasons I don't understand, God put blinders on the doctors so they didn't find his illness.

My husband has told me he feels Joe around. That seems right, since Joe, out of my three children, seemed to get along best with my husband. They had so many similarities, but there was never much communication between them because they could both be a little pigheaded. Since Joe's passing, my oldest son and his father have become much closer.

I still have some contact with some of Joe's friends. His passing affected many of them very deeply, and unfortunately changed their young outlook a little bit. But they still say hello and they still remember Joe in their hearts.

I hope when it's my time to pass on, Joe will be there to greet me. I want a big hug from him, because my son was a hugger. When people talk about what they miss most about Joe, they tell me they miss the hugs. I do, too. Whenever he saw me he would give me a hug, and get me laughing. I know that when I see Joe again, he'll tell me, "It's about time you got here!" Something to make me laugh. Or, "You have to see the girl I met here!" Something to shock me. But that's my Joe. And I can't wait for that day.

THE SESSION

"If you're all set, let's begin and see who comes to visit. Okay . . . well, a male presence comes to visit. Actually, three. And a female as well. In that little group over there, there's talk of a young male [who] passed on."

"Yes."

"He passed over young by today's standards. Just so I can get this out of my head, there's talk of a 'granddad' being with him. I'm not sure if it's his or yours, so don't explain. But there is talk of an older male there, like a grandfather."

"Yes."

"The younger male is being referred to as the son that passed. He says, 'son slash brother.'"

"Yes."

"Actually, yes, he does come as the son passed on, so I take it he's your son. And I take it that he's not your only child because he speaks of a sibling. And . . . he does call to his dad also."

"Yes."

"He's calling out to you as his mom, and he speaks of a brother."

"Yes."

"He also says brother and *brothers*, but the latter being in the term-of-endearment sense. Like friends who are like brothers."

"Yes."

"He also speaks of a grandmother being with him."

"Okay."

"From his point of view—and don't read between the lines—but he kind of felt he could have been closer to his dad."

"Yes."

"Because he brought him up, gave me the impression that you might find that surprising, and then extended an olive branch. And that would tell me that there was a gap-of-communication type of relationship. But the extension of the olive branch would be to close the gap on his end."

"Yes."

"Obviously he and his brother are very close. Understood?"

"Yes."

"He reaches out to him not only as a brother, but as a good pal. And he does so because he definitely . . . he knows . . . that in regards to his passing, he knows his brother suffers in silence."

"Yes."

"Now, they come to you, assuming you know what they're talking about—so let me just say that he reaches out to his brother and just hopes his brother understands that he could not have saved him . . . that there was nothing he could have done. Hopefully his brother understands the meaning behind that, because I don't want to put words in his mouth. He does speak of a tragic passing."

"Yes."

"Yeah, he also . . . don't explain anything . . . he talked about being near home, like he's going home or going from home to where he was supposed to be. But he does talk about it definitely being an accidental passing."

"Yes."

"A *momentary distraction?* Understood?"

"Yes."

"But one thing he does state, at least for everyone's benefit—he is all right and in a happy, safe place. He does thank you for praying for him in your own way. He's not religious or anything, but it does embrace him with your love, and you can feel like you're still doing something for him. And . . . this has nothing to do with religion, but I see the Blessed Mother reaching out to you, as one bereaved mother to another. So I hope that makes sense to you. One thing that's interesting—he just wants to make sure that you know he didn't suffer at the time of his passing. Understood?"

"Yes."

"I don't get the impression of him passing instantly. He has, so to speak, a few minutes or so before he officially passes on."

"Yes."

"And he thanks somebody for being good to him prior to his passing. I keep seeing out of the Gospels the story of the Good Samaritan, understood?"

"Yes."

"So apparently somebody provided nurturing comfort prior to his passing."

"Yes."

"I don't know if you know the person or have any contact with him, but he definitely expresses gratitude for somebody's kindness prior to his passing. So, in any case, he does call out to this person in appreciation, because somebody definitely showed compassion. Interesting . . . he gives me the impression that this was . . . hmm . . . it was all part of a much bigger picture. He states that it's . . . I'm trying to think of how to state this . . . it's like your son, in another lifetime, did the same thing for this person that this person did for him. So it was kind of like . . . *karmic* . . . to give the other person the opportunity to do the kindness that was done to him in another lifetime. Very interesting. But the main thing is that because he didn't pass right away, he wants to make sure you know he wasn't suffering at the time of passing, because someone is showing compassion to him. This person was like a guardian angel to him—to help put him at peace because he made the transition. He does admit that he was kind of shaken and a little scared at what was happening. But he does say there was no one at fault and nobody to blame—it was a genuine accident. But of course, it brings heartbreak to you all, his family. In a general sense, so that nobody feels left out, he does call out to friends who he would call *family* as a term of endearment, and he speaks about a big turnout at his wake and funeral, understood?"

"Yes."

"He says that there might have been people there that even to this day you don't know, but knew him."

"Yes."

"But . . . even though [it was] a short life as we would understand it, he still insists he had a fulfilling life. He states that you feel like you didn't have the opportunity to say good-bye, but as he brings up, there are no *good-byes* here—eventually you're going to head that way just like everybody else, and he will be there to welcome you over.

"Somebody was definitely helping him to cross over. But again, as he says—which is so interesting—it had to be. Because the same thing had happened in another life, where *your* son showed compassion and nurturing to this individual who was on his way out.

It may not have been necessarily an accident—it could also have been illness or something else—but the paths had crossed once before. And it's not like this person and your son are great friends or even know each other—it's again, like the Good Samaritan, it's somebody he didn't know, but *did* know in another time. He says it's one big wheel with many spokes. Also . . . I saw Saint Joseph appear—which is a symbol that in spite of the circumstances, it was a happy passing. Saint Joseph is the patron of a happy death. But also he appears because of the name, too, understood?"

"Yes."

"He calls out to family to tell them you've heard from him. He does know that his brother definitely got rattled by this. He does call out to his brother that he's around him very much like a guardian angel. But he wants him to understand that he can't fix everything in his life for him. And again, with regard to the fact that he wasn't sure that there was a hereafter, he's here to say yes, there is, but ultimately everyone has to learn that for themselves. Even in this experience right now—some people will believe it, some people won't, but he's not here to convert anybody. Ultimately, we'll find out for ourselves. But he also jokes that when the day comes and he welcomes all of you over, you'll all find out he was right as usual."

(She laughs.) "Yes."

"He's not too worried about it. Complete confidence. Again . . . speaking about this other person, I take it you still have contact, or you did?"

"Yes."

"He calls out again with expressions of gratitude, because he gives me the impression that this individual may feel he didn't do a big deal, but as your son states, the simple, sincere things turn out to be a big deal over there. He also states he has come in dreams.

This is not the first time you're hearing from him. Before you've spoken to me, you've already had evidence he's near. Also, too . . . you may feel as though you've seen him."

"Yes."

"There's that feeling that there has already been an apparitional experience, which is really the top-of-the-line in visitations. As he states—it was the *real McCoy*. He says sometimes you feel like you might not get enough signs from him, but yet you talk to him all the time, which actually is a sign. You are feeling his presence—you already know who he is because you're his mother—and that feeling prompts you to speak to him. The same with his brother."

"Yes."

"And again, he does tell me that he did have a fulfilling life. He does speak of grandparents—without saying anything, I'm sure some have passed, but he still has some here. This is a big shocker—you don't expect to outlive your child, but certainly a grandparent wouldn't expect to outlive a grandchild."

"Yes."

"He says you've gone through the worst and you're living with the worst. And then he jokes with you with regard to his brother . . . he says mother but don't smother."

(*She laughs.*) "Yes. I understand that."

"He says that he knows it's the only thing left. You may have heard of tragedy happening to people more than once. He knows that a lot of times when his brother goes to work, you hold your breath."

"Yes."

"But he doesn't at all give me the impression that his brother is going anywhere any time soon."

"Good."

"This has nothing to do with religion, but I keep seeing Our Lady of La Vang appearing in the room here, reaching out as one bereaved mother to another. She's one of my favorite apparitions, and it's probably why she's showing up like that. She says you've prayed to the Blessed Mother . . ."

(She is unsure how to answer.)

"They bring up that you're maybe at times a little *pissed off* with them over there."

"A little."

"That's normal. And maybe 'pissed off' is a little strong—maybe the better word here is . . . *disappointed.* That [you] might have never really expected much help from them, except for the best for your children, and to protect them and so forth. And then this happens, and it's a *big* letdown. But your son says that they don't have anything to do with it—that everybody is on their own unique journey, and apparently his reached its conclusion. Again, that feeling . . . his encounter with the other person, because of what happened in another life . . . history had to repeat itself, that had to be done. But it's the same feeling, even in the other lifetime, when your son did it for him—they didn't know each other. They were strangers. But he expresses gratitude to this other individual, so if you have any contact and he's open to this, you can let him know. Don't explain this, but I feel like I just heard the name Jay or Jason."

"Yes."

"Without telling me, because your son called the name . . . I don't know if it's the other person or somebody close to him—I don't know . . . but your son called out the name, and I hope you understand."

"Yes."

"He hopes you'll sleep better tonight. And again . . . he just wants to make sure you know that he wasn't afraid to pass. He knows at times you've been afraid of him being afraid."

"Yes."

"Don't be alarmed by this, but he also impresses you to keep alert to your health. More so in the emotional sense."

"Yes."

"I don't mean to laugh, but your son just said, 'You can keep your comments to yourself.' "

(She laughs.) "Yes."

"He's right. I can get very skeptical about this. Losing your son, *anybody* could tell you this. But he tells me, *Anybody didn't say it, I said it.* So okay. Sorry. He's getting a little testy with me, but also doing it for the fact that he's actually a sweetheart and he's using humor so you'll know it's him."

"Yes."

"He knows you have your days. He knows you wish that things would *hurry up.* But he says you're not supposed to be there yet, and just keep in mind every night when you go to bed, tell yourself *one day closer, one day less.* There's no conception of time over there . . . so for him, it's like you're coming tomorrow. Even though for us, that's not the case. Eventually, when you do pass on, you'll actually feel as though he left in one moment and you followed in the next. He seems like the kind of guy who would find his way and make friends very quickly."

"Yes."

"He definitely settled in. He kids with me that yes, he knew he was going to pass on, and when he got there he needed to get to know the neighborhood. He seems to have found his way there very nicely. He just doesn't want people to feel he was cheated out of his life the way we would think, because of his young age. He fulfilled his journey here. One thing he does state, though, when he looks into this world from over there, is that he doesn't miss all the *bull* that goes on here."

(*She laughs.*) "Yes."

"I can't say I blame him on that one. But he also brings up for you to remember to comfort yourself with knowing that you have a child who is completely all right and in a happy, positive existence. You don't have to worry about him. With that, I think he's going to pull back—boy, he doesn't waste any time, he got right to the point. But certainly, he asks that you continue to pray for him, and he calls out to family and his term-of-endearment family, friends, and so forth—again, that he's all right until we will meet again, which eventually will happen one of these days. He speaks of you working . . ."

"Yes."

". . . which he's kind of glad you do. He's concerned about the fact that you may think too much. (*She laughs and agrees.*) The thing is—maybe you thought you should take some time off and be home for a while, but he's trying to deter you from that. He's afraid that if you have too much time to think, that's exactly what you'll do. Whether you hate your job or not, it does have its therapeutic purposes. It distracts you."

"Yes."

"Plus, it's a sign of life moving on. Again, each day is one day less and one day closer, until we meet again. He speaks of pets passed as well."

"Yes."

"They were there before him. Which I'm always happy to hear. They were there to help welcome him over, and that contributed to making it a happy passing, because they instantly put you at ease. But in any case, he tells me he needs to pull back, so I shouldn't fight it by trying to hang on. But certainly, he embraces you with love, and calls out to his brother and dad, friends, the one he was seeing—all the people he left behind—and wants to assure you all that he's all right and in a safe, happy place until we meet again. And with that he pulls back, and the others do, too, and there they go. And away he went—but just from me."

Stories like this always fascinate me, and for different reasons. First, I love to hear about the world-within-a-world the souls help to create so that nobody feels abandoned at the time of their passing. It's also very clear with stories like this that there are simply no accidents on the earth. When they are needed, the souls will move heaven and earth to get somebody where they need to be in order to help us to help ourselves, even if it is to help ourselves transition to the world hereafter.

Another reason I found this story so fascinating is that the souls rarely want to mention reincarnation. They have a fear that they will be misunderstood about why we come back to the earth after the joy and beauty of the hereafter. One of their fears is that it could potentially be possible for a soul to have reincarnated to another life before we have the opportunity to see them again. This is a common fear among the bereaved, and I am glad to have yet another opportunity to tell people that it simply does not happen.

The souls do not and will not come back to the earth in what must be a heartbeat of time, even if it means as much as fifty or sixty years of our time. They just barely had time to get there and enjoy the fruits of their hard work in *this* lifetime—why on earth would they leave so fast? They don't. They won't. They also continue their education and spiritual growth in the joy and beauty of the hereafter, so nobody there is in any particular hurry to get back to the perils and pitfalls of our world. But they do occasionally tell us about different lifetimes to help us understand that we as people are much more connected than we think. Joseph was absolutely right when he said as a young boy that strangers are just friends we haven't met yet. Many souls on the earth are people we may have interacted with in another lifetime. Sometimes the roles change, and always the circumstances change, but they are still souls we know, if not consciously. It just helps us to understand that the pattern and fabric of each of our lives is not so random as we may have thought, and that kindnesses done in one lifetime can have far-reaching results.

5

I SHOULD HAVE KNOWN BETTER

SARAH ZIERING

The human mind is the center of our physical universe, and this center creates beauty, understanding, and love within us and for the rest of the world. In many ways, the mind is to our physical being what God is to the souls—the source of all energy, hope, peace, and joy.

Just as the mind can be used as a tool of greatness within each of us, it can, sometimes, be a weapon we use against ourselves. It is possible to destroy all beauty, thought, and harmony with a series of unhappy and unhealthy thoughts. What the mind has built up within us, it can use to destroy us. When this happens, due to circumstances both within and beyond our control, we run the risk of falling through a door in our journey that we may never be able to come back through, literally killing the heart and soul of our very existence. In past sessions, souls have told me they "died of a broken heart" or that they "gave up," but this circumstance was peculiar in both the way it happened as well as the fact that it happened to someone who should have known better. Some stories like this don't have a happy ending. Fortunately, this one does, and I was pleased to play a small role in the soul's journey back through an unintended door.

I have known Sarah Ziering for many years, and I consider her one of my best and most trusted friends. It seemed that destiny had a hand in bringing us together.

I unknowingly "met" Sarah one night at a group session, where she accompanied a patient of hers who was having trouble coping with loss. Even if she introduced herself afterward, I wouldn't have remembered—after a night of souls coming and going at breakneck speed, all needing and wanting to reach out to family, the faces of people on the earth just seem to blend together. Show me a soul who talked to me, and *that person* I will remember. But people on earth? Not so much.

The day after the program, we got a special-delivery package to the office. It was a case of wine. With the wine was a beautiful handwritten note on fancy cardstock. It read, "Thank you for your kindness and for helping one of my patients. You are truly extraordinary. A gift of *spirits* for the spirits. Sarah Ziering, MD." We saved the beautiful card so that I could write a thank-you note and include a prayer card for the woman the souls now prodded me into remembering was Sarah's patient.

Two weeks later, we had scheduled a Family Grief Weekend, during which we spend an entire weekend with bereaved families. The program featured notable speakers and grief counselors, and included a session with me for each of the families. We found out just two days before the weekend that our grief counselor had broken her foot and would not be able to speak at the program. I immediately thought of the note, and asked Andrew to call Dr. Ziering to see if she might be available that weekend, since she was local. As a psychiatrist I knew she could speak volumes about the physiology of grief, and as luck would have it, she was willing and able to help us out.

To know Sarah is to know a woman with many hearts. She can be as objective and intuitive about spirituality as she can about science. There is no modality she will not explore for a patient in need, and she is one of the most erudite and articulate people I have ever met. Honest, compassionate, and generous, she once told me with absolute seriousness and no irony at all, "George, you can do in ten minutes what it might take me ten years to uncover." What was begun that Saturday has become a friendship we have both often relied upon in the years since.

Sarah has had many sessions, and in different circumstances over the years, but this particular session stood apart. This session was going to be about her—not facilitated by her, and not moderated by her for somebody else. I wanted her to hear from the souls something that would benefit her directly, and not just relatives with salutations, an ax to grind, or a message for somebody else in her care. This would be all about Sarah. Some years ago, she was ill with cancer. She put on a brave face at the hospital, but I knew she was terrified. In her room at St. Francis Hospital, she managed to get on her feet to greet me despite having had major surgery just a few days before. I looked at her carefully and noticed something very odd about her: she seemed to be glowing, as if something were covering her in a beautiful veil of protection. I turned to Andrew and said to him, "I wish she knew." And he asked, "Knew what?" And I answered what the souls told me: "That she's okay. She's okay, only she can't know it yet. She needs to heal. She's got a long road ahead."

This is Sarah's story, in her own words:

I was born in New York City, and was raised by a single mom. My dad was seriously psychiatrically ill. My parents met at Columbia University; from there, my dad went on to law school, and then they married. And they got pregnant pretty quickly after they got married. My dad had had a little bit of a depressive history before they were married, but I think having a kid was more than he could handle. He developed . . . I'm not sure exactly what it was . . . schizophrenia, bipolar disorder . . . something bad. Basically, it got triggered by my mom getting pregnant with me. So that was the beginning of his undoing. Their marriage fell apart. He became seriously psychotic and crazy, and she had the baby. My grandparents did not have a lot of money, but they told my mom to move home with the baby and get a divorce. But even with the approval of her parents, she became the black sheep of the rest of her family, and his, for having done that. His family didn't want the divorce—they wanted her to stay with him and take care of him. Meanwhile, he was stark raving mad, and my maternal grandfather, who really saved my life, told my mother she couldn't leave him with a baby while she went out to support us. My grandfather was worried that my dad was so sick, he might throw me out the window. So they divorced, we moved to my grandparents' house, and my mom went to work. She really struggled—she was a single mom, she was a disgrace in her family for getting a divorce, and besides her parents, nobody on either side was very sympathetic. And she was very bruised emotionally by him getting sick, because she loved him. But she had to struggle on her own now with work, life, and a little girl. When I was three years old, my mother had saved enough money to move us back into New York City.

There were things I loved to do when I was a little girl: I loved to draw, I took dance class, and I loved the arts. I had a series of infections, though—kidney infections and throat infections—and had to have my tonsils taken out. My mother went from doctor to doctor to try to figure out why I kept getting these infections; finally, she happened upon a homeopathic doctor. The doctor was a tall, very regal, elderly lady with silver hair arranged in a bun. She examined me and then told my mother to take me off milk. As soon as my mother did that, all the infections cleared up. Even at my young age I was quite taken with this doctor and her ability. I thought, *I'd like to do that. I'd like to be the doctor that kids come to who is able to figure out what's going on and set things right with them.* She was an early and big influence on me. I didn't think at the time that I wanted to be a doctor, necessarily, but the image of her stayed in my mind.

When I was seven years old, my mother remarried. He was a wonderful Italian Catholic artist. I adored him, and he adored me. He was everything a lonely little girl could want from a father figure, and he was always there for me. He loved my mom and he loved me. But a year and a half after they married, he developed testicular cancer and died. My mom got incredibly depressed after that—she was now 0 for 2 with husbands. She also tried to help fill the void with me after his death—I got a kitten and then a puppy. She did whatever she could to cheer me up. She also decided to enroll me in private school. This private school was very artsy—they did a lot of drawing and painting, writing, and music—so it was a great school for me. Although I loved anything artistic, I also loved my science classes. I thought science was pretty cool. My mom really tried to give me everything she could—private school, summer camp, travel—and she was a member of the Gurdjieff Foundation, which was a very spiritual type of school. The Gurdjieff Foundation, with their focus on arts, spirituality, intelligence, self-awareness, and knowledge, was the underpinning of my young life.

I did well in high school and got into Harvard. Even though I was very artistic in high school, I decided I wanted to study science when I got to Harvard. Even though I loved the arts, I felt the disciplines were very subjective. There was always a lack of objective truth. With science, there is always an answer, and science is very resolute. I thought I wanted to do science research because I had a friend from high school who had become a science researcher, but when I started the research track, I found I didn't like it so much. It was lonely to sit in the lab by yourself all day long. So I thought about pre-med, remembering the holistic doctor I had loved as a little girl, and I could really see myself becoming a doctor and helping people. So I took the pre-med requirements and majored in biology. I ended up getting into Harvard Medical School, so that was pretty cool. I didn't really know I was interested in becoming a psychiatrist, but when I did the clinical rotations through the different fields of medicine, I found that my interest and passion was in talking to people and helping them with their emotional issues.

I hadn't seen my dad since my parents' divorce, and as I got older, it started becoming more of a hole in my life. I think part of the reason I found psychiatry so important was the influence my father's mental illness had on my life. I got into St. Vincent Hospital's program for psychiatry, where I did my internship and residency, and I started to think, *What if my dad were to walk into this emergency room as a patient? What if he walks in after twenty-five years, and I have to take care of him?* It started to bother me that I hadn't seen him in so long, and no effort was ever made on his part or his family's to see or find me. I started making inquiries in my family, but nobody wanted to tell me where he was. But I always had this strong feeling every time I was on the Upper West Side of Manhattan that he was near, and with my mom's help we were able to search some public records for him. And I found him—he was staying in a run-down single-room occupancy hotel, where he was living in filth, almost like a vagrant, and dressed in rags. My next project was to get him on his feet and gain his trust. And I did—I undertook a whole rehabilitation project to get him well, and he did. I continued with school, met the man whom I would eventually marry, graduated, and then set about starting a family of my own.

My best friend growing up was a girl my age who lived in the same apartment building as me. She and I were in the first grade and her brother was in kindergarten. The three of us were the closest of friends. Jeff and I always hit it off unbelievably well. He was funny and cool, and cute, and he adored me. She was my best friend, and he was my best friend. I always had a bit of a crush on him even though he was a year younger than me, and I knew he liked me. As we matured, it was pretty obvious to people that we liked each other. As I got older, my mind starting thinking along the lines that it might be nice to go to the next level with him. He was very much like a soul mate. When it came time to go to college, I had gotten into Harvard and he was in his last year of high school. So when it came time for him to apply to colleges, he was accepted to all three of his first-choice colleges, including Harvard. When he got all his acceptances, he called me and said, "I got into all the top schools—where do you think I should go?" And I told him to come to Harvard, thinking this could be our time together to begin a relationship. His sister was hoping he would go to Yale, where she was enrolled, but he chose Harvard. I told her that I was so excited that he was coming, and she told me, "Sarah, please—don't sleep with my brother unless you intend to marry him, because he loves you." That carried a lot of weight with me because she was my very best friend. He came from an Episcopalian family, who, although they adored me and I ate dinner at their house more often than my own, were very outspoken in their views about not wanting to associate with Jews. They were upper-crust WASPs and very concerned about their social standing, so they had some very parochial views about certain people. It was odd and sometimes crazy—they would be completely snobby to my mother, a single Jewish mother, but at the same time love me. But they did make it clear a number of times that with regard to their children and marriage, being Jewish was a big problem. That's why the thought of potentially marrying into that family, even though I had real feelings for Jeff, was going to be very difficult, combined with the fact that his sister made me promise I wouldn't be intimate with him unless I thought we would end up married. I had relatives who just barely survived World War II, ran for their lives, and part of my mother's family had been wiped out by Hitler and Stalin. So in my mind, this was impossible. To keep things with Jeff from going any further, I brushed him off when he came to Harvard. And as a result of that, he stopped talking to me.

I met my husband when I was a fourth-year medical student. I had to push Jeff out of my mind even though I missed him terribly—I still considered him one of my best friends. Through his sister I would occasionally see him, and the three of us would still have a nice time, but I knew deep down that he was mad at me. I knew why he was angry, but I pretended I didn't know. I suppressed my feelings enough to allow myself to meet somebody else. And I did—a handsome guy who was a great doctor and a talented pianist, and Jewish. I was head over heels for him, and he loved me madly. I was gushing one day to a fellow psychiatric intern about my new beau, and after listening to me go on and on, he said to me, "You know the one thing you haven't mentioned? You haven't mentioned that you love him." And although I defended myself and my love for him, I did find it interesting that somebody should pick up on that. But I did love him—of course I did. We eventually married, and Jeff did come to the wedding because we were still considered friends, and I invited his entire family. My husband and I had a little apartment where we invited people to come after the wedding to celebrate with us as we opened wedding gifts and had champagne. The last person to leave was Jeff. It was me, my husband, and Jeff sitting there, until my husband told him it was time to go. He reluctantly got up and said good-bye. And that's when it happened—when he got up to go to the door, I felt my heart just break to pieces in my chest. It was clear to me at just that moment just how deeply I had hurt him.

The first years of my marriage were wonderful. We were a great team and very compatible. But what I began to realize about my husband was that he had a certain level of self-involvement where he just couldn't feel what other people were feeling. He had a "me first" attitude that came from being the only son in his family. He could be arrogant and narcissistic, qualities I hadn't noticed before we were married. It became especially apparent when my first son was born. My son was nearly a year old when my husband's dad, a man who was almost obsessively connected to his son, died. It's almost as if my husband transferred this obsessive bond to our son. Although we had three more children, none came close to the kind of bond he formed to my oldest son. It was starting to bother me a bit, not only because it became obvious to the other children, but because I felt I had also been supplanted by this relationship. I started to feel like an afterthought. One day I confronted him about it at a restaurant. He had a bit of a temper that would cause him to get really angry at times, even in front of the children, but he was not the type to make a scene in public, so it was safe. We talked about his obsession with our eldest son; the fact that he didn't know my favorite color, or my perfume; the fact that he thought that because all his needs were met, we had a perfect marriage. The conversation took an unexpected turn: he told me he hated his life and that he needed to do something for himself because he found no fulfillment—he wanted to work on theatrical productions as a musical director. So because I wanted to make him happy and our marriage a success, I moved heaven and earth to help make it happen. And it did—he directed a musical at our local synagogue. It was a great success, and he was very happy.

Next, he had the opportunity to become the music director at the school my children were attending. The job seemed perfect for him, so I encouraged him to do it. The director of the show was a young woman about twenty years his junior, and she was definitely the kind of woman he thought was pretty. Basically, she was my physical opposite—blond, blue-eyed, perky—the kind of woman he would point out to me on the street as his type. He became seriously infatuated with her, and it became the only thing he liked to talk about, even at home. At first it seemed innocent, but it started to become very invasive in our lives. But I knew he loved the theater program and he was doing it with our kids, so I reluctantly allowed it to continue. Between my husband's infatuation with my son and now with this young woman, I was starting to feel hopeless, as if I were sliding down the list of importance. There was so much to do in the running of our family's life, and it all seemed to fall on my shoulders. I found myself just trying harder and harder to keep it all together, for the children, for the house, for my husband, for my own work, but it felt like a losing battle. Nothing I did seemed to make much of a difference to him. I tried saying something to him about the fact that he talked incessantly about this woman and all the fun they had together at the theater. I know he wasn't sleeping with her, but he seemed to have lost all interest in me and everything else except his own interests. He blew up at me and it turned into an ugly, nasty scene.

I remember being in the shower one morning and thinking about what would happen if I got divorced. Thinking about having to raise four children on my own, just like my mother had had to do with me, and about how my husband might turn the children against me for divorcing him, I started to panic. I knew what being a single mother was like—I'd grown up with one. And I knew what it was like to be completely abandoned by a family, be-cause it had happened to *my* mother. I was completely out of hope and started wondering if there was a point to continuing, here, or at all. I thought, *I should just get cancer and die.* Everything seemed to be going wrong, and I was unable to see any alternative to my terrible situation. I started feeling like I was trapped. I know I was being emotional and of course didn't think I could ever wish ill on myself, but I started to think back on that morning when, just a few months later, I started feeling very tired and showing some symptoms of illness. I knew that something was very wrong.

I was diagnosed with colon cancer that had metastasized to my liver. The doctors told me there was nothing they could do about the cancer in the liver, and I remember feeling as if I was sliding down a rock wall with no handholds. I was going to die, and there was nothing to hold on to. I was given a 50 percent chance of sur-vival. When I told my husband, he was furious with me. He was angry that as a doctor himself, my illness made him look bad some-how. He treated it as though I had made a suicide attempt. Like this was all my fault and it was inconveniencing him. He told me, "This is always harder on the spouse than it is on the patient," and I thought, *Really? You're the one who has to go under the knife? You're the one who has to get chemotherapy? You're the one who's going home with a port in your chest? This is harder on YOU?* He was not a big help in the next few weeks. I went through surgery to remove the can-cer from my colon and liver and six months of chemotherapy—a very tough regimen right after a very tough surgery. But during the surgery, something happened that changed everything—I felt I had a near-death experience. I felt myself leaving the earth, and I remember thinking, *Well, I guess that's that.* But when I got to the place I was going, whoever was around me looked concerned. *You're not ready yet, are you?* one of them asked. *No*, I said out loud. *I don't want to die. I can't die. I have a bar mitzvah to arrange for my son . . .* and just like that, I started feeling some pain as I woke up from the anesthesia after the surgery.

I didn't want to die, so I had to find a way to live. I decided if I was going to try to survive this, I needed to clear my conscience and remove any negativity in my life. I wrote letters to people I felt I had wronged and made calls to people I may have not been the best to. I also knew I had to square my conscience with Jeff, because he never knew why I had pulled away from him so many years ago. That whole situation still weighed heavily on me. I remember sitting on the bedroom floor trying to wrestle this whole thing out of my guts. I had brushed off this boy because of so many things—my mother, his mother, his sister, his family, my family—everything under the sun except for one thing—because of anything that *I* felt. I couldn't have predicted whether our friendship would have gone on to marriage or not, but the *Jewish husband* thing was so firmly planted in my brain, I couldn't see down the road to know what the right thing to do was. But it was clear that life had a different plan for both of us. I told myself I had to call Jeff and apologize and tell him the real story, regardless of what he made out of it. We were still friends, and we were still cordial. We talked for a very long time. He did not want to acknowledge in the conversation that he loved me back then, but I can understand why. He's also married and has children—but I remember so many times when it was made clear that he had real feelings for me. I told him about my feelings, and I told him about why things had happened as they did, and that it had nothing to do with him. After I spoke, there was a long silence on the phone, and then he simply said, "Thank you." And I know he heard me.

I cleared my conscience of every possible thing I could think of in my life, and now I knew it was time to clean my soul. The night before chemotherapy, I went to the mikvah–a ritual bath of purification in the Jewish tradition. And I prayed to be healed. I didn't want to die–I realized I had made myself sick, but I didn't want to die, not now, nor even that day in the shower. I was just stuck, and hopeless. I decided to do whatever God wanted me to do. In the mikvah I had an extraordinary experience–after being inspected and making sure I was perfectly clean to enter the bath, I looked at the pool and saw that there was no water in it. I asked the attendant when they would put the water in, and she said, "Look, the water is in there already." The water was so clean and so clear that I literally couldn't see it. And I knew that was a sign that I would be clear.

Some months after my surgery, George Anderson wrote me a letter. He said he was concerned about me, and that he had had a dream that involved the Virgin Mary. In the dream, he told the Virgin Mary, *I'm worried about my friend Sarah,* and the Virgin Mary told him, *She's in the clear.* It was the exact word I had seen as a sign in the mikvah. She told George that she offered a prayer on my behalf, and she gave George the text of the prayer. George wrote that he asked the Virgin Mary how to tell Sarah who she is, since I'm Jewish and the Virgin Mary is a symbol of Christianity. She answered him, *Just tell her that it's the Lady from Lourdes.* I said the prayer he transcribed in the letter every day, and even had it printed up so I can see it every day in my bedroom. He also sent me another gift, a statue of an angel, who I found out later was

Metatron, which he told me my guardian had instructed him to send. It is one of my most cherished possessions.

Since that terrible time I have been cancer free. I have also felt a huge sense of accomplishment by not carrying any pain or secrets anymore, especially the pain I carried about Jeff. I feel clear. *In the clear*, like I was told. I've addressed cancer and I've addressed the issues with Jeff, and I decided that for my own peace, I had to address the problems with my husband head-on. Up to that point, I was trying too hard to be supportive and understanding, and all the while I was losing myself—and almost my life—in the process. I confronted him, and initially it did not go well—he went completely crazy. But this time it didn't affect me because I was much stronger and much more aware of the cost of my just folding, forgetting, losing myself in the house and family, and not living for me and my needs, too. I got myself into therapy, and I'm standing up for myself. My pattern of always capitulating is over, and the change has done a world of good. Gradually, over the past couple of years, things have gotten better, and we are working together as a couple again. I feel like I've come a long way now, and there are things in my life I know I want to pursue for myself. I love what I do, I love helping people, and I love my family. What will come my way? I'm not sure, but I know I have a reason to live—and it's not about psychiatry, or romance, or family—it's about serving God. Where He needs me, and when, that's where I, and *my* life, will be.

THE SESSION

"Okay, let's begin and see who comes to visit us. Hmm . . . I'm sure you're not going to be upset by this, but so far, only an angelic presence has come forward. I'll be honest with you—there may be family and relatives, but they seem to be holding in the background. As the individual says . . . it's a male . . . the best way to get me to understand is to refer to himself as an 'angelic presence.'"

"Is it a guardian angel?"

". . . Yeah, because he says you needed one. (*She laughs.*) Right across the board. It seems he has a sense of humor, because he says you *needed* one. Over the last several years. Interesting . . . he says you're starting to break away . . . not that you're a selfish person—you were always trying to keep everybody else happy. But now, you're starting to make yourself happy first . . . nothing wrong with that. He says you listen to everybody else's problems—who listens to yours?"

"Yes."

"This is not being said in a negative way—even with family you've started to break away. There are some days you've had it up to here with your own family. He states—and it may be a justified feeling—that you're always bending over backwards for family, and feeling unappreciated."

"Yes."

"Including youngsters. I don't mean to laugh, because he uses an old expression, but he tells me you're not everybody's 'chief cook and bottle washer.'"

"Yes."

"He takes me back to when you were ill. That you had been internalizing anxiety, feelings of lack of appreciation. There was part of you feeling that you'd had enough, but didn't know what to do about it."

"Yes."

"And I'll be honest with you—this is interesting—he tells me you could have passed on from your illness. But you had an experience we would consider a near-death experience."

"Yes."

"The experience helped wake things up for you. You were presented with the opportunity to either stay or to go. And he definitely tells me—if you said you'd had it on the earth, they would have said, 'Okay.' But it was *you* who said you wanted to go back."

"Yes. That's exactly what happened."

"Funny . . . he says that's why you got well. He tells me that as much as you had made yourself ill, you also were able to heal yourself. It wasn't a bolt of lightning, but it did set the stage for wellness to happen—you started going in that direction as soon as you decided to come back."

"Yes."

"He says you were going through a very lonely time as well. He brings up that even when you were sick, you were between a rock and a hard place. Again, a time of anxiety, but many worries about what you were going to do. But you made the choice that was right for you—to continue on the earth."

"Yes."

"And things have gotten better. There definitely were some dark times, but . . . it's funny—he states that these probably aren't the things we think we're going to learn, but you actually had to learn to stick up for yourself. And the thing is—sometimes we think that everything should be cut and dried—and he says that sometimes our beliefs, our religion, can mess us up a little bit. Sometimes religion can be a troublemaker."

"Yes."

"He also says you might not have recalled completely in your near-death experience that you were shown that if you go back, this is what will be in your future. You may not remember, but they state that they showed you, if you took this direction, this is what will come to pass. You had to find yourself."

"Yes."

"You know what—to be honest with you, I believe this guardian angel to be Metatron—the chief archangel among guardians. Either it's him or one of his minions. It's part of his circle. He's definitely around you. A lot. But it's interesting that he doesn't care for the title I gave him. He just wants to be considered a guardian. I'm not sure what to do with this, but he shows me the Book of Enoch. It's one of the stories in the Old Testament they took out. Enoch became Metatron. This is the same person who came to me to send you something after your illness, which, as it turned out, was the same person you were praying to. So he answered."

"Thank you."

"Also . . . he tells me the reason why you had the specific trouble with cancer is that you were sending your anxiety there—to your gut . . . because of having so much anxiety, you actually compromised your immune system. *(She nods.)* It seems that the heart of your illness was in your gut."

"It was colon cancer."

"I just saw Saint Jude appear, who is the patron of those in hopelessness or despair. It was a desperate situation. Even now, sometimes you feel you're still knocking your head against the wall?"

"Yes."

"But also because of your experience, you've also been able to heal yourself. Physically *and* emotionally. You may feel at times that you're still sometimes knocking your head against the wall, but now you're kind of letting some things go in one ear and out the other."

"Correct."

"A lot of times, as the souls state—it's not wrong for us to say that something is not my concern. Or it's something you cannot involve yourself in. I see Saint Teresa of Avila appear, and she says that sometimes it takes more courage to stand back and let the person or persons find it out themselves. Not that you're not close to family, but there are gaps . . . there is a little bit of you having had enough with some people."

"Yes, definitely."

"I wouldn't be surprised if up ahead, you took a trip either by yourself or with a good friend—it would probably do you a world of good. I'm getting the feeling from the souls that you're traveling up ahead. And that you're telling those around you that you need time for yourself. According to the souls, you don't relax enough. Even now. I mean, you're not going to make yourself sick again, because that was your wake-up call. They also talk about your diet— you need to watch the quality of food that you eat. (She nods.) I also hear the name Mark called."

"Yes. My brother."

"They mention congratulations around him."

"Yes."

"He will hear—or has just heard—some happy news."

"Yes."

"Funny—work wise, I see him going out of the country."

"Yes. He's working on a project that will take him out of the country."

"They show him traveling—that this year and the next will be big highlight years for him. Efforts put forth are definitely being rewarded."

"Definitely."

"Your angel friends are back. You and your son are having a big lack of communication?"

"Yes."

"They're telling me you can't make heads or tails of him right now. *(She nods.)* My head feels as if it's spinning, and I'm hoping when it stops that it faces the front again."

"Exactly."

"He's at a rebellious stage right now. I know he's a grown man, but they're kidding me that he's acting like a teenager."

"Correct."

"He's being rebellious, and . . . looking at you like you are interfering too much in his life. They're telling me you have to back off a little bit. They're showing me a pulling back of the reins, so you may want to back off a little bit."

"Definitely."

"This has nothing to do with formal religion, but Saint Teresa of Avila appears and says that sometimes it takes more courage to back off. There's tension between you two."

"Exactly."

"One soul over there tells me—in a complimentary sense—he's scientific but he's going overboard."

"Yes."

"He's much too *black and white*. And you can't tell him anything, so it's not even worth it to try. Like the souls say, he's got to learn it for himself."

"Exactly."

"The souls give me the impression he's starting to feel a little unsophisticated with regard to his religious beliefs, spirituality . . ."

"Yes."

"Interesting. The souls say things aren't 'science' because they just haven't been proven yet."

"Exactly."

"Also . . . the souls bring up that he's a little frightened by spirituality—his own and in general."

"Ahh."

"Fear on the earth is the worst of the negativities here. Just like pride was the worst of the Seven Sins. From fear stems all the other negativities."

"Yes."

"And he has this fear right now. Fear of spirituality. Fear of ridicule. And from that stems all the others. He's afraid of being afraid."

"Yes."

"He's a little addicted to fear right now. And it can be an addiction."

"Thank you, that's very helpful."

"There's a female from the other side telling me to tell you to just *let sleeping dogs lie*."

"Okay."

"You don't have to challenge. Just agree to disagree. Not to be condescending. He's entitled to his opinion."

"Exactly."

"He's seeing someone? Somebody who may not be who you want, but somebody there is warning him to be careful on this one."

"Yes."

"And she's not helping with his state of mind right now. They're a little concerned for him right now. He seems to be wanting to be a follower and not a leader. But right now is not the time to say anything. It will just backfire. Again, he's got to learn it for himself."

"Yes."

"The souls also bring up your relationship with your husband. They say it's better, but not entirely . . ."

"Right."

"Again, that feeling I get from them that you've had it. (*She nods.*) They say you definitely need time to yourself. You need a break. You're trying to be a professional, a wife, a mother . . . and you're getting a fight out of it."

"Yes."

"It's just that home life is very tense right now. (*She nods.*) They tell me you need more rest. You're not . . . harmonized. You're not in harmony with yourself. Make sure that if you let something go, you really let it go."

"Yes."

"Don't be alarmed, but they do make mention of your health again. They express concern about your health, but not in the way it was before, like what you've already gone through."

"I understand."

"They give me the feeling I'm running on fumes."

"Yes."

"They tell me you're thinking too much. And they're telling me to tell you to put that in check. It's funny—it's like you need to be out of the house. You need something to keep your mind occupied and to get out a little more."

"Yes."

"You definitely need some rest time. Also . . . not only that, but if during the day you're alone, take naps. You need rest."

"Will do."

"You need your mind clear and you need rest. They state that you need to completely turn off for a little while."

"Yes."

"They know your heart's in the right place—trying so hard to take care of a family, but this is the rabbit hole you fell down into the last time. They say you're not responsible for anybody else's problems. Nor can you fix them."

"Right."

"Just recognize right now that it's a transitional time and a sensitive time for kids who are growing, and you, who is changing."

"Yes."

"They show me the *Titanic*, which is my symbol for *every man for himself*. Right now, it should be everyone to their own issues."

"Okay."

"I heard the name Jeff, too."

"Yes."

"Somebody called out the name. He's here on the earth?"

"Yes."

"The souls talk about him finding understanding. There are also health concerns around him. But it's around him, like it hasn't quite manifested itself yet."

"Okay."

"Again, the souls are telling you, though, to keep things to yourself, and not necessarily share everything with your family right now. Like this session."

"Okay."

"I'm being told by them to watch yourself emotionally—it's easier said than done, but they're telling me you have to relax."

"Yes."

"I keep feeling I'm in ten different directions. You're trying to do everything at once."

"Yes."

"I see your dad. He's telling me you're not responsible for everything here."

"Okay. How's he looking over there?"

"Just fine. But he says sometimes you just have to be told directly—you're not responsible for anybody else. You can't lead anybody around by the nose, nor would you want to.

"This is . . . this is a little strange. He doesn't expect to be recognized. He's telling me he's Sigmund."

"Sigmund?"

"I don't recall ever seeing this before, but I saw Sigmund Freud appear behind you."

"My gosh, really?"

"There's just a feeling of him being around you. Probably because of your similarities, professionally and otherwise. He's interested in your work. He's giving me the feeling that he was a very liberated individual. He compares your sense of responsibility to a nearly tragic circumstance in his own life."

"Really."

"He jokes that *ooooh*, the Nazis would have loved to have gotten their hands on him. I know they did get members of his family. They would have loved to have gotten him."

"Of course."

"There are many people there who are helping you to help yourself, but they can't do it for you. Cecile, or Cecilia—she's a motherly presence who is also a guardian to you."

"Yes. My grandmother."

"She's closer to you than you can imagine. There's one thing they want to summarize for you—you're in *no man's land* right now. So you can only put your best foot forward—for yourself—from now on in. (*She nods.*) And they're telling me you're feeling a little trapped. Don't make the same mistakes twice. You fell down this hole once before—they're here to make sure you don't do it again."

"I understand."

"But with this I get the feeling they're going to pull back. They impress me again for you to research the Book of Enoch. Many people are invested in your continued wellness. It's important, and the angels who are invested in your life are very important."

"Oh yes."

"Continue to pray to the guardian angels. They tell me your prayers are being heard."

"Good."

"I see the Holy Spirit over your head, which tells me you are blessed. And your father is telling you to listen to what everybody here has told you."

"I will. I definitely will."

"And there they go."

I feel like I have to walk a careful line with this story. I want to help people, but I don't want to cause panic. So here goes: it is possible to make yourself sick. And yes, it is possible to end your life without ever picking up a weapon. This happens when the soul becomes so hopeless it has nowhere else to go but from whence it came, and the body begins to suffer and die. This is one of those doors you can be blown through by circumstance or push yourself through by will, if that is what you want. Nobody wants to die—in theory. But nobody wants a sick soul, either. It can only happen if we allow it. It can and does happen if we let people take from our soul without a way to replenish peace and hope. It's like a well, and sometimes the well can go dry. But sometimes, digging into a dry well will produce another flood of water—but we not only have to want it, we have to be willing to do the hard work it takes to dig, and dig, and dig until we find the source.

I have to admit that as well as I know Sarah, I didn't actually know her personal struggle or the extent of the pain it caused her. Sometimes sessions are a real window into the personal lives of people, and both they and the souls spell things out, not for shock value or to exploit some very personal things, but to help provide insight. As much as I was sorry for Sarah's suffering, I am proud of her for telling her story, and allowing the souls and me to help understand the whys and hows, and to take the information and use it to her own benefit.

The decision to live is always our choice. Just like we cannot survive without oxygen and water, our souls cannot survive without peace and hope. But I am a big believer that when you create peace and hope for others, you also create it within yourself. We have far more power than we believe we have on the earth, but it's a tool we need to learn to use with care. The best part is that whatever we create with this power is ours to keep. Forever.

6

THE FAIRY GODMOTHER

GREG WAYNE

Free will is a wonderful thing. It allows us to see with our own eyes and forge ahead under our own steam. It can also be a bit of a bitch. Free will allows us to let our fear run amok in our lives, and to have the past influence the present and the future. So free will, like the proverbial free lunch, is a bit of a misnomer. Nothing that confines us is free, and nothing that stands in our path is free. We use our free will most often to create problems that simply don't exist, or to find answers when there was never really a question. But we are perfectly within our rights to believe what we want to believe and call it our will. Our *free* will.

A curious thing happened one day when Andrew came by the office and we happen to get onto the subject of Greg, an author who believed his house was haunted. Andrew told me that Greg lived in a turn-of-the-century home on Long Island, and I, being a bit of a history nut, wanted to see it. We found an image of the house on Google Maps. It was lovely—a typical Long Island Colonial. And then I looked closer and became more than a bit intrigued: in the image, the shadowy figure of a woman can clearly be seen sitting on the steps in front of the house. *Now that's interesting,* I thought. I wanted to know more about the woman in the photo, why this "ghost" was in the house, and why she had gotten such a bad rap over the years. Greg was kind enough to sit for a session, and it turned out to be quite the eye-opener.

This is Greg's story, in his own words:

The house I live in, one of Long Island's Farmhouse Colonials, was built in the early 1900s. Our family moved into the house when I was six or seven years old. Growing up, there were definitely moments when weird stuff happened around the house. By this I mean we would hear strange noises in the attic, and even stranger noises going up and down the stairs when I knew there was no one on those stairs. There would be the sound of breaking glass in certain rooms, but no broken glass. Sometimes we would go outside to see if somebody had thrown a bottle at the house, or dropped something, or even if a basement window had been broken, but there was never a discernible reason for the sound. It was as clear and loud as somebody smashing a pane of glass with a hammer right next to your ear. And I wasn't the only person to hear it—my sisters would hear it, too.

The mysterious noises were just one of the many challenges my parents had at the time. They were in their late teens when they got married, and they had me before either of them had even turned twenty. Their relationship was tumultuous; they were just too young for all the responsibility they had. They did their best, though. My father worked long hours, sometimes eighty hours a week, and my mom was working fifty hours a week. They didn't see each other much, and they didn't have a lot of energy left at the end of their workdays. In fact, any energy they did have after a long day, they turned into anger at each other. Now, this didn't happen every day, but often enough that it wore everyone out. They wound up having a lot of kids, so the stress of all those children and my mom and dad literally working day and night caused their relationship to fray at the seams.

Needless to say, there was a lot of tension in the house when I was growing up. At the same time, there were a lot of phenomena happening. Looking back, I realize I didn't yet have the vocabulary to describe the things that were happening—and maybe still don't. The sounds, the feelings, the presences that could be felt. Very often I could feel that *something* was there—there was no way to really articulate it. But you could *feel* it. Sometimes it felt like there were eyes on you, just watching. My mom, who was quite empathic throughout her life, felt that there was a lady in the house, someone who had likely been there for a long time. She didn't feel the spirit was aggressive or mean—she was just *there*. For my mom, it was as if there was another quiet person in the house. As far as I know, my mom never talked to her or engaged with her, but she did acknowledge the presence. That's how strongly she felt it.

Fast-forward a number of years. I'm married and living with my wife in a small town not too far from where I grew up. My parents had divorced, and my mother wanted to sell the house. I was apprehensive. It did make sense to buy it, even though I had some ambivalence about returning to what I felt was "the scene of the crime," where there weren't a lot of happy memories. My mother wanted to start a new life, and that meant getting out of the house and starting over upstate. My wife and I didn't really have the money to buy the house at the time, but somehow we applied for a mortgage, got it, and became homeowners.

In the beginning, I felt like a bit of a failure. Here I was, in my thirties, moving back to the place I grew up. I felt like it was a step back. But after some time I decided it didn't have to be like that and came to the realization that yes, my wife and I could be happy in the house.

We spent a lot of time gutting the house and doing renovations, so we didn't actually move in until six months later, when most of the house was livable. For about a year it was just my wife and myself, and sometimes we would feel that presence in the house. We used to joke that there was a ghost in the front room watching us as we watched TV. Even though the first floor rooms are all connected to one another, they are separated by French doors. Every now and again, I would look at my wife and say, "Doesn't it feel like somebody is looking at us from that room?" And she would respond by saying she had just been thinking the same thing. Nothing frightening, nothing scary, just weird.

One night there was a blackout. My wife and I were sitting in the living room, where we'd lit candles. I said to her, "You know, if that ghost is here, she'll be able to make that candle dance." And I swear, maybe it was a coincidence, maybe it was a draft in the house, but that candle flame started jumping around as if it was excited. Knowing that anything can be the cause of a dancing candle flame, I couldn't help but think this was a pretty wild coincidence to have happened the exact moment when I made my joke. Not lottery odds, but still.

Other than the occasional noise, things were relatively quiet in the house after that. We had our first son about two years after moving into the house. But a few years later, after some personal struggles, things got . . . well, interesting. It started out feeling like the presence that had been there since my childhood, but then things escalated. There were noises at all hours of the night coming from nothing that we could see. The house somehow felt electrified, with snapping and crackling noises very much like static electricity. We started hearing footsteps up and down the stairs, strange noises in the attic. Things would fall unexpectedly. We both would see things out of the corner of our eyes, and there was a palpable feeling of some kind of presence in my son's room. An electrified sensation would course through my body when I entered my son's room. My wife was starting to feel a presence of somebody walking right behind her. These strange things began happening on a regular, almost daily basis. I recognize that it's an old house, and old houses have noises and sometimes also electrical problems—but the frequency with which these undeniable events were occurring was unsettling. The strange events in the house lasted for about a year and then ended.

At the same time, I found myself struggling to cope with the stress of work, home, and family. Interestingly enough, it was also one of the most fruitful times for me spiritually. I started meditating and praying, and I found myself doing it regularly. I began to feel as if God's presence was with me, and things seemed to make more sense and become more connected. I truly believe that the period of inner solitude, deep prayer, and meditation I was having in the morning may have opened me to other things, other realities, and other presences around me.

In retrospect, I look back at that time as not so much "the year of the scary ghost story" but rather "the year of the incredible spiritual journey." While everything was going on, I was perplexed and frightened at times. If there was something in the house, I wanted it out. I tried to get rid of it. But, I didn't have the vocabulary to understand what was happening and I may have let fear get the best of me. After the fact, I started to see the experience as a positive one.

We still live in the house. The phenomena have mostly subsided, but occasionally something will happen—not to the degree it did before, but just enough to remind me someone is still hanging around.

There was a lot of pain in that house while I was growing up, but there was a lot of love, too. I can't forget that. My parents are good people, and they worked really hard for the family. My dad and I are estranged, unfortunately—I haven't seen him in years. But I still keep in touch with my mom.

In college, I was moved by the play *The Oresteia* by Aeschylus. It's about the fall of the house of Atreus, and how bad decisions and revenge create a constant cycle of hatred and sadness. The end of that play is all about stopping the circle of sadness and abuse in a family. Looking back, I think we bought this house in part because there was an opportunity to change the past. To end a cycle. We grew up with a lot of tough stuff, but here was an opportunity to redeem the house. And, perhaps, ourselves. Perhaps whoever was in the house was trying to help us accomplish that.

THE SESSION

"Okay, so let's begin and see what happens. Okay . . . somebody's just telling me to follow what I'm hearing. So I'm thinking *all right, all right, whoever you are.* A male presence comes forward so far, and comes as family. The real McCoy, so it's actual blood family. He talks about dad. I take it that dad is passed on."

"Not that I know of, but . . ."

"Oh, okay. Maybe I jumped the gun. He's out of your life? Let me start over again because I think I jumped the gun. A male presence comes forward in a fatherly manner. But then he talked about your dad, so I assumed he was your dad. So if he had passed, you would have heard?"

"Yes."

"Okay, then this must be a grandfather, coming in fatherliness. Then he talked about dad, so I started to jump in that direction. And then I realized where I went wrong. He told me he wasn't there, and I thought he was trying to tell me he's passed on, that he's not with you here. But then, when there was hesitation, he said yes, there has been a death, but in the emotional sense. And that's the mistake I always make—they tell me the person is not there, so I'm taking them to mean the person is passed. So I jumped the gun from what I was hearing. So it's true your dad is not around— he's not in your life. This must be going on for a while."

"Yes."

"So your granddad states that there has been a death, but in the emotional sense. . . . Not that he's trying to be insensitive, but you're kind of used to it."

"Yes."

"Your grandparent gives me the impression that you didn't have the easiest upbringing. There are people around you who give me the feeling that they are parents, but in the grandparent sense. There's a feeling from them of knowing your mom's side better. So they're more on the maternal side. They brought up that you didn't have the easiest childhood. It certainly wasn't *Meet Me in St. Louis*, that's for sure."

"That's true."

"They say you basically came from a dysfunctional home. They're pointing at me, because I know exactly what they're talking about. And also, they reflect that in life you've dealt with a great deal of disappointment, understood?"

"Yes."

"They state your mom is here, on the earth."

"Yes."

"Again, some gaps in communication? I hate to say this, but whoever brought it up told me that in some ways she's here and not here. Let me stop for a minute and say something that is coming through. I don't know who this is—and I don't want you to say anything—but there is a lady around you who does come to you as a mom. It's not your biological mother, because they told me that, and it's not a grandmother, either. Somebody—I don't know what to call her—somebody who sympathizes with you, because things hadn't gone as a youth the way you expected. I really don't know what to make of her, because I don't get the feeling of her being blood kin. But . . . 'family' is used very lightly over there—it can also be used as a term of endearment. She gives me the impression that she is around you like a guardian angel. So that's what I'll call her—your angel. She gives me the impression she hangs around. Wherever she was when she was on the earth, she liked the life and was content with it. It's like she's not ready to move on just yet. Not that she's bad or anything like that—she's just . . . to be honest with you, it's as though at a point in your life she's your adopted mom. She adopted you spiritually because she saw the crisis you were in, in the emotional sense. You've had your tough times emotionally. There's just a very nice nurturing and compassionate feeling coming from her. It's as though she just touched me in a soothing way, and I suddenly *tingled* from it, feeling very secure. She brings up that even though your mom is on the earth, in a lot of ways you kind of felt like an orphan. And it feels to me that this presence always wanted to have a son. It's funny—you must have felt her around. She's not threatening or anything like that—I actually feel very soothed in her presence. So I hope you do also. She talks about your mother also dealing with a lot of emotional struggle. I keep getting the feeling I'm being tossed around in a boat. And growing up you might have felt that way."

"Yes."

"It feels like growing up you might have felt like you didn't have anybody . . ."

"Mmm-hmm."

". . . in regards to actual family. They were here, but they weren't here. She shows me the book *David Copperfield*. If you recall in the book, when David's mother passes on, he doesn't have much of a life, but eventually his aunt takes him in. And that's the feeling I get from her—she's like a godmother. Now, without telling me anything, she gives me the impression that where you live now, she lived there at one time."

"Yes."

"I don't know if you know the history of where you live, and I'm trying to be careful that this doesn't come across as some kind of haunting scenario or anything. I don't know who she is, and you may not know, either, but I feel very comforted in her presence. And apparently you have also."

"Okay."

"But she has—bear with me on this—she seems to have some

kind of connection to where you live now, or where you grew up. She's somebody who passed over, but never really wanted to move on. She seems to have been very comfortable. It seems like you felt her around for a long time."

"Yes."

"It's like somebody who came to your rescue. I know for a fact that no force is exercised over there, so she could have gone into the light, and then decided that she was happy where she was and that she wanted to stay there. I see you as a child and she's there. She's very sympathetic to the fact that you feel you never really had a family. One thing she does tell me, too—you're very sensitive. She brings up that you were kind of a lonely guy growing up."

"Right."

"She's like somebody who is a godmother to you. She stays around. She's not trying to be funny, but she says she's like a fairy godmother."

(Laughs) "Right."

"She's trying to put it into human terms as best we'd understand. It's funny—and I'd love to know if she ever lost a child when she was here or something—but she just likes being a mom. She likes being a motherly figure to you."

"Okay."

"She kids with you that at times you might have felt you were haunted. But not in a negative sense by any means."

"Mmm-hmm."

"There's this feeling that throughout your life, you've always known somebody was there. Especially when you felt you were like an orphan. But I don't get the feeling she's related to you in any sense that I could understand. And really, a godmother doesn't have to be a blood relative. And at the beginning I started to challenge her a little bit at first, but she reminded me that *family* doesn't always have to be by blood, and just because somebody is blood family doesn't mean that you always like them."

"Right."

"But she mentioned, which confuses me, that she has lived with you. But I'm thinking it's the other way around—did you live where she lived? There's just such a nice feeling with her—her presence in the room is very soothing. And you have felt it, so none of this is new. She shows me you as a little boy crying and upset, and I can feel her soothing you. Whoever it is says no, you haven't lost your mind."

"Okay."

"That's the thing that I find so intriguing—that she obviously was so comfortable in her life when she was physically here that she just decided that she's not in the mood to move on yet. And nobody forces you in the hereafter. And in her sensitivity and kindness, [she] felt very much for you and just decided, *This is where I'll look in.* I guess you'll have to do some research into where you live to find out who was there beforehand, because there's the feeling that somebody there has seen her. Maybe you, or . . . she gives me the impression that she's made her presence known."

"Yes."

"And yet, not to be frightening or anything like that. Nothing like that at all. She seems very simple—there is an essence of naïveté with her. And not to mean that she's mentally diminished. She just says to me she only sees the good. And she can recognize that things aren't always happy and that things aren't always good for someone else. And it seems like she's come to recognize that even though she doesn't really want to move from this situation, she still feels she's doing her job. It's not like she's wasting her time here. She must have been a very patient person, took life as it came—I wish I could take up her characteristics—she never got angry . . . and even though she's a grown woman, there's the feeling with her that she's childlike. And again, where you grew up—where you felt her presence—it's an older home, so other people have lived there before. . . . When she was here, her life was very simple. And [she] is thrilled to know that even when she passes, she doesn't have to go anywhere. She can just stay. It's odd—you can't really confirm this, but she seems to be telling me her name is like Annie or Alma. She brings up that you were brought up in a bit of an abusive home."

"Yes."

"She's not capable of judging anybody because she only sees the good, but she tells me your mom could be a tough cookie and your dad flew the coop."

"Yes."

"Again, things didn't turn out there the way they started out. And there's that feeling that as a child you may not have felt you had anybody to turn to, understood?"

"Yes."

"And you're also not that enthusiastic about turning to anybody here. So she senses that and just fills that gap. She doesn't mean this to be harsh, but she says you're a very complex person. You have tremendous inner struggle. And as she states, so much of it is from childhood, some of it is from the present. Sometimes you just don't know what the hell to do with it—you don't know how to handle it. She can't take over your life, wave a magic wand, and make things go the way you would like, but she's just giving you a reinforced feeling."

"Right."

"I'm actually getting the chills from her presence, because there's nothing there but genuine goodness, thoughtfulness, kindness—there's just nothing but positive reinforcement coming from her. And the thing that's interesting [is] she somehow has reached that spiritual level and is happy with it. It's just the way she likes it. I also see animals around her. She might have had pets. And again, that goodness around her. That's the thing—I don't know if her name is Anna or Alma, but it sounds very close to that. As she told me, and not to be conceited, but she says she has angelic qualities. She also gives me the feeling that she also had her struggle here, just like you—although she says that all in all she had a happy life. She's just not capable of doing anything wrong. It's that simplicity about her. People who knew her here may have thought she was simpleminded. But it's not the case. She also felt a little neglected by her family when she was on the earth. You grew up in an older home?"

"Yes."

"Again, the roots of all of this are in that home. The one you grew up in, or the one you live in now. Or both. It seems like other people also felt her around—or saw her there. I get the feeling from her that she's an adult, but she's childlike in her thoughts and actions. There's that feeling of shelter—she either had a sheltered life or a sheltered upbringing. Actually—was your residence built in the 1920s or before?"

"Before."

"Okay. I felt like I was going way back, but then I saw 1920 and before that, but that also may be when she was there. It would be interesting if you could do research on that house. She still lives there, so she had to have lived there before. You don't have close ties with family of your own, understood?"

"Yes."

"And as she states, you're still trying to find yourself. She says, 'Don't sell yourself short.' You internalize a great deal, and there's that feeling of internal struggle. Also, not that she's putting anything down, but religion has kind of messed with your head a little?"

"Well . . ."

"She says that . . . one of the greatest difficulties you have is trying to keep everybody happy. Well, I can tell you were brought up Catholic."

(Laughs) "Yes."

"You're inclined to be a people-pleaser. That's okay, but you should try to please yourself as well. She says at times you feel you are living a double life.

"Your sensitivity is a great trait, but it can be a troublemaker. And it goes way back. And it's funny, she gives me the impression that even though you're a grown man, it's as though you never went past a certain age inside. Like at times you might feel like a ten-year-old. There's a feeling of trauma with you from your own family, where your growth stunted emotionally. If you feel cornered or mistreated or something, the little boy is the one that gets upset, and you'll react."

"Yes."

"Even work-wise, there's feelings of disappointment . . . you're still kind of a kid inside. And this is probably another reason why she hangs around with that soothing motherliness. Your mom has also had her struggles here."

"Yes."

"And you might have felt that you are caught. Between your mom and dad. You keep your distance when it comes to family?"

"Yes."

"She gives me the impression that's maybe not a bad idea. They're still trying to find their way here, too. And at times it may feel like the blind leading the blind. Also, she gives me the impression you may have held yourself back career-wise, almost thinking like you're not capable, understood?"

"Yes."

"She encourages you to get out of that thought process. You may feel like you're only good enough for *this*, or *that's* just fine. Sometimes you are inclined to settle . . . and there's another part of you that doesn't like that. It's almost like the little boy inside struggles with the adult.

"Even without telling me, if you have a sibling or siblings—*family* doesn't exist for you in the way we've been brought up that it's supposed to. It's just strange with this woman—either she lost a child, or she always wanted to be a mom and couldn't be . . . she's just very innocent, and in her innocence wanted to love and care for somebody. She does bring up that you . . . prayed out there to whoever it was."

"Mmm-hmm."

"Because it's almost like in a way, you invited her. Which I think in that case means that you didn't have an objection to her. And I think that's why she says she picked up the thought or the light from you, and figured, *Well, this is for me.* But also she seems to have witnessed in the home what you might have been going through. The souls have all the time in the world to hang around until they want to leave, because time doesn't exist [for them]. She says that a lot of times souls will stay or go back to where they were happiest for a time. In her case she seems to be content there.

"It's not like she didn't cross over and acknowledge that she had passed on—she just wanted to go back to where she had been happy and also, then, recognizing the predicament you were in, figured she could do something nice here. She's just a fairy godmother—a guardian angel. She says that somebody doesn't have to be related or biologically connected to make something like that happen. She also cautions you to watch for a tendency toward depression."

"Mmm-hmm. Okay."

"She's diagnosing that for a good deal of your life, you've been dealing with what psychiatrists would call a *masked depression*. It's been there for a while, probably since childhood. It's been there so long that you don't know anything else. So your attitude is like, *That's as good as it gets—this is the way it is.* However, the symptoms will manifest in defensiveness, impatience, crabbiness, bouts of anger and frustration—it shows itself every now and then. Not that you're not a nice person, but again, it's almost like you're not really fully understanding that it's there, and it's all you know. She very gently speaks to you about masked depression and anxiety, and you don't have to tell me anything, but she counsels you that it might not be bad to seek professional help if you haven't already. There's nothing to be embarrassed about—you're a person who's sensitive, and you're allowed to have your feelings. If you haven't already, she encourages you to get in touch with that little boy in there.

"Even growing up, she gives me the feeling that you have

friends, but you don't have friends. You might have been picked on, made fun of—again, that feeling that you're trying to play the game but they won't let you join the team. It does feel like you've been a loner your whole life. You're social, but you're awkward with it. You're like me—you get the party invitation and you think, *Oh God, how do I get out of this?* That's the first thing that goes through your mind. [But] if there is something that you can genuinely say [is] why you can't make it, you're thinking, *Thank God, I'm clear.*"

"Ha! Right on."

"Again, she feels it would not hurt for you to seek professional help. It doesn't have to be everybody's business. She knows you'd rather handle things yourself, but she also knows you're a private person with the world around you. If that's what makes you comfortable, then do things in a private way, without the whole world knowing about it. She talked about that you have your own family. Child, children, that sort of thing?"

"Yes."

"I didn't think you did, but she told me not to assume anything that I think I may know. She does compliment you that you are a good dad. Because the experiences that you've been through, you don't want your children to go through them. So again, look upon how you grew up not in a negative sense all the time, because it's helped you become the person you are. And as a dad, she says you could have gone one way or another. You could have gone the not-so-pleasant way, like what you experienced. But she compliments you that you stopped the buck from being passed. So she knows you are a good dad. I mean, you might have your days—everybody does. But you yourself are very understanding, soothing, and you've taken up paternal qualities where your sensitivity has taken on a unique role. So that's why it might be hard for you to understand—she says sometimes you might want to look back and look upon your upbringing as a lesson in disguise. Because if we learn for ourselves, we learn it forever. She says sometimes you can be your worst enemy, though. Be careful, because you constantly get in your own way. And don't say anything, but you have a very deep sense of being knotted inside—there's that part of you that internalizes things. But she says that the things you feel very deeply about are your business. That's the way you like it, and that's the way it is."

"Right."

"This is interesting . . . probably because of his extreme gentleness across the board, I saw Saint Francis of Assisi appear behind you. He comes as a guardian saint. He is definitely somebody you can pray with to help you help yourself. He understands because of his gentleness with animals. It's funny—you considered religious life at one time?"

"Yes."

"Yeah, because Saint Francis appeared again, so this may mean that you were attracted to the Franciscan order, or just religious life in general. Ehh—it wouldn't have been for you."

(*Laughs*) "Right."

"They say that because you might have looked at it through rose-colored glasses. And they give me the impression that you might have ended up going in and wondering how did you get yourself into this, and being unhappy. You can be a loner, yes?"

"Yes."

"That's the thing. I know you have a family, but still you need your space. There's nothing wrong with that—that's how you are.

But what is so nice to hear from her is that you're not an abusive father—you try to be very patient, and she knows you're doing your best to be the model dad. I see a swift right curve in front of me, so apparently you've gone in the right direction. It's interesting how she puts this—you may desire change or movement within your work, but yet part of you likes the status quo. So there again is another struggle. You may want to advance or progress, but you start thinking maybe you should leave well enough alone. The thing is, as she states in a very soothing, motherly way . . . you need to ask yourself, *What makes me happy?* If you can honestly say to yourself that the status quo makes you happy, then you know. If something's not broken, you don't have to fix it. But sometimes you may notice that the grass is getting greener in the other guy's yard, and you may feel you are being left behind. And you'll have to come to grips with that yourself."

"I understand."

"I see a spider web in front of you, which is my sign of a very complex person. But also be careful—a lot of times you're frightened. Sometimes the people in your family may not understand—you're a very private person, and even though they're not pushed out of your life, you're still needing time by yourself to put pieces back together. She brings up that even your wife understands that sometimes she needs to leave you alone. Obviously [she's] a very understanding person and just figures sometimes to just let you breathe. But once again, she states that you are in the driver's seat—you have to learn it for yourself like everybody has to. You have to find what works best for you, even if it takes time."

"Okay."

"But I think with this she's going to pull away. This was kind of interesting, because nearly all of the sessions I do are with family, related family members. But this woman is not kin, but definitely comes as family. It feels like she's been around you since you were a little boy. It's like she found you, growing up in the house she lived in, that she never really left and she wanted to take care of you—it's what she wanted to do as her spiritual work. Everybody finds what's best for him or her when they pass on, and she chose you. But she certainly embraces you with love. There are other relatives over there, but they . . . they're not connecting. They're not being mean from over there, but this woman had the need to speak. But she embraces you with love as a godmother. A guardian angel. Again, this feeling that you're not going to feel whacked-out knowing that she's there. She's your godmother, and she likes it. She's not pinning any medal on herself, but she's very happy to do it. She says that people have such a wrong perception of the souls. They don't always have all the answers, but they can help. And she will be there to help. And with that, she signs off, and there she goes."

I'm not sure Greg expected to have some rather personal things come to the surface via his "godmother," but he was gracious and generous about the fact that it had happened. I think when these personal things were put into perspective, especially by the souls, they are not as difficult to understand. The souls understand us, our world, and our motivations, struggles, and human frailty. They were us once, too, and they continue to carry their humanity about them in order to fully understand ours. This woman had tried so hard to help Greg help himself, even when he was trying his darnedest to get rid of her. But she didn't take it personally, and perhaps she understood that in trying to rid the house of her, Greg was trying to rid himself of the past—of hurt, frustration, and pain. In a way, she did haunt Greg: she brought bad memories to mind. But when we face our past tragedies and draw strength from them rather than letting them have control over us, our ghosts have nowhere to go but back into our imaginations.

Some time after the session, I asked Greg if she was still making her presence known, and if it still bothered him and his family. Greg was quite honest in telling me that no, she was not as active in the house as before, and in an odd way, he kind of *missed* her. The lady is still there—I know it. She's just biding her time until she can help again, in another circumstance, in another time. I didn't want to rattle Greg, but his kids are growing, and their terrible teenage years are just around the block. He's going to need all the help he can get.

7

GOOD MEDICINE

KEARA BARNABY

I often think of our life's journey as a hallway with many doors on each side. We may walk directly through this hallway in a fairly straight line, but sometimes, one of those doors will open, and we will be called by the person on the other side to help them on their own journey. We are not always called to another door on the earth. But if we are, are we able to heed the call? We can pass by and miss a valuable life lesson, or we can walk through the door and into the adventure of another's life circumstance. These stops may be brief, but they become defining moments in our journey on the earth. They create a great, and very specific, opportunity to grow in our spiritual education on the earth.

I met Keara Barnaby one night at a birthday dinner Andrew threw for me at a great little French place in Huntington, Long Island. Keara is easy to remember—in addition to being beautiful, smart, and funny, she has blue eyes that shine like diamonds. Though I thought I had just met Keara for the first time that night, she reminded me that we had, in fact, met a few years before. She had come to a group session, which turned out to be a reunion of sorts—she reconnected with Andrew after many years, and she reconnected to her birth father, who left the family when she was a little girl and had since passed on.

Besides having a background in music, Keara worked in medicine—oncology, to be specific. We talked about how our jobs are both on the spectrum of life and death—hers, before they pass, and mine, afterward. She spoke so enthusiastically about her work and how it's a tough job but a fulfilling one, and I was curious to hear if there were any times she seemed drawn to a particular patient whose passing she would not forget. I wanted to know if there was ever an occasion that her own journey here was sidetracked briefly by the needs of another human being who had wandered, seemingly accidentally, into her life. With so many patients nearing their own passing, I was curious to know if her path had ever caused her to stop, like a motorist on a highway, to help another person who was stranded by the side of the road. But before she could answer, we were interrupted in the most beautiful way—desserts. French desserts.

Because I am so easily distracted by sweets, I never did get the answer to my question. But when it came time for another book, I remembered Keara's background, and thought it would be fascinating if she were to sit down for a session and see which patients would come through to thank her for her care and commitment. She was amenable to the idea, and although it was an open field for me, I suspect Keara already knew who would come through, and why.

This is Keara's story, in her own words:

I always loved medicine. My interest in going into medicine as a career was sparked by my grandfather having colon cancer and helping to take care of him. When I initially went into medicine, I was in internal medicine, but after my first child was born, I discovered a love for oncology. I work as a physician's assistant. It's basically like being a doctor—I can do the things the doctors do for patients, but my work is overseen by an MD. I started out in a part-time position, but in 2002, I went into oncology full-time. I found that it really was my calling, and what I wanted to be my life's work.

Oncology is a very comprehensive specialty. It's fascinating from a scientific perspective, and it's multifocal—you really have to be able to balance all a patient's medical issues within their cancer, and also along with their cancer diagnosis. Some people who have one cancer may also have other comorbidities. So it helps to have a really strong background in internal medicine in order to succeed in oncology. And aside from the medical aspect of it, there's also a very strong personal aspect. Part of what I do within the treatment of cancer is help transition people to hospice when their diagnosis no longer responds to treatment and becomes terminal. Even though the survival rate for cancer is much higher than it was even twenty years ago, there are some patients whose cancer may progress, even after years of treatment, and some whose cancer will progress quickly despite the best treatments. Part of what I am able to do for my patients is help them accept the process and the outcome, whatever it is—and that is the part I really focus on.

I love the medicine, but what I really love is the interpersonal aspect of the patients and their care. I help them understand their diagnosis, their illness, and, when the time comes, their transition into palliative care. Sometimes patients need help accepting that medically, there is nothing further we can do for them. It helps them to know that the medical team they have entrusted their lives to cares about them and all their issues, and this also helps the patients' families. We give a lot of support and guidance, and help patients understand the process when they are dealing with end-of-life issues—that we are not going to allow them to be in pain, and we are not going to let them suffer. And after having fought so hard, sometimes patients almost feel they need permission to let go when their time comes, and that they don't have to fight anymore. We try to make it okay for them.

I also find myself having to step in, in a very personal way, when patients have very little support in the way of family and friends. When they are facing these issues alone, it's sad and very scary, so they will very much depend on you not only for treatment, but for love and support. When that happens, you become a family member to them—they open up about their disease, and they open up about their fears. You really come to know a lot about them and their lives—their successes, their failures, their loves, and their tragedies. It all comes together, and with you, things can come full circle. You experience their life through their eyes. You experience their illness through their eyes. At the point where we can't do anything else, there comes this acceptance of the whole concept of life, and sickness, and dying. And you become part of their acceptance—you helped them find it, and you help them through it. And that becomes their moment of peace.

I feel myself called upon more as a friend sometimes than a PA, especially with the really sick patients. They're scared, and they need a friend more than a doctor at that point; they just need some-body who understands. At the point where we cannot do anything more for them, they don't need any more diagnoses; they just need a friend and maybe a hug. Although we try hard to help save their life, when that can't happen, then the next best thing is to be there for them in any way they need you—and sometimes that just means holding their hand. So while the patient is making a transition, the medical personnel around them are also making a transition—we go from treating them the best we can, to understanding them as best we can, to just being a friend when it is needed. Together, we accept the limits of medicine, and we all transition to the next phase, which is to help them to understand, accept, and, when it's time, let go.

I met Hedda when I was still doing internal medicine. I had not flipped over to oncology full-time yet, but I was working on the on-cology floor. She came in with acute leukemia, so she had a lot of in-patient procedures, and sometimes her counts would plummet and she would not be allowed to leave the hospital. She needed constant transfusions and was often at high risk for infections. Since this meant I would see her for weeks at a time sometimes, she and I became very close.

After a series of treatments, she did really well and was able to go home. She was out of the hospital and feeling well, and she would invite me to her home, where we would have a great time. But then the leukemia came back, and she knew it wasn't going to be a very long illness this time. We started to talk about what that meant. She confided in me that she was terrified of being alone when she died. She felt very alone in her life, even though she had more friends than she could count. She felt very insecure and unloved. In our time together, both as a clinician and then as a friend, I promised her that she would not be alone. I tried to make it okay for her to accept the reality of her condition, and I know part of her acceptance was feeling better about the fact that when the time came, I would be there to see her through it and stay with her to the end.

I really got to know Hedda in a personal way. She didn't like to talk too much about her life, but from what I gathered in the scant times that she did, it was a troubled life. She was not accepted by her family because she was a lesbian, and although she did have many friends and a few romantic partners over the years, she found herself being used very often by the people she trusted and considered her friends. Because she was very generous and wanted so much to be loved, she was not always the best judge of character, and she would lavish both attention and money on anybody who wandered into her life. Unfortunately, most of the time this backfired for her, and her good nature was taken advantage of. It caused her to become so distrustful of people, and caused her to feel very alone. I never remembered seeing any family present when she was in the hospital for such long periods of time. Family was a subject she didn't want to talk about, even though she was very open about everything else in her life. I don't even know if she had any brothers or sisters, or living parents. She did have me, who she considered a good friend, and not only did she trust me, but she felt very safe with me.

It was during this time that I found out I was pregnant with my first child. We were both elated. Both in and out of the hospital, we talked about the baby, and it was a great distraction from her troubles at the time. But one morning she called me at home and told me she had a rash that was causing her some pain. She had it checked out and learned that it was shingles. My heart sank—shingles is a viral infection caused by the reactivation of the chicken pox virus, and it is very dangerous for pregnant women. Hedda was now back in the hospital, and I had to explain that because of my pregnancy, I would not be allowed to visit her. I knew she was upset, but I promised I would find a way to be with her when things became acute and she was starting the process of dying. I had enormous guilt that I couldn't be near her as her illness progressed. When I promise something, I hold that very sacred and I make it my business to keep my promise—especially to people like Hedda who count on me so heavily. But I had to worry about the health of my baby. I called many times a day to make sure she was okay and that she was comfortable, and hoped she understood that it was just out of my hands to be able to sit with her. But I was with her in spirit. To make matters worse, I found out that I had placenta previa, a condition where the placenta is too close to the cervix, and that it was bleeding. I was put on bed rest for the remainder of my pregnancy. There just seemed to be no way I could keep my promise to Hedda that I would be there with her when she was dying.

Right around the time I was confined to bed rest, Hedda took a turn for the worse. Before that, she had been calling me to give me updates on how she was feeling, but she suffered a transformation of her illness from a less acute form of leukemia to a fulminant relapse, where the symptoms are sudden and dramatically more severe. She didn't last very long after that, and she died, I was told, in her sleep.

One of the nurses from my floor called me to tell me. But she didn't have to—I knew. I could feel it, and I knew she had passed away. I could just feel that she wasn't here anymore. I can't explain it, but it is something I feel from time to time when my patients pass. Sometimes I will wake up from a sound sleep in the middle of the night and just know that a patient I was close to had passed within that hour. And I can go into work the next day and not even have to be told that the patient passed. Not with every patient—I think I would go crazy—but for the ones who were special to me, like Hedda—yes, I absolutely feel it when they pass.

Near the end of my pregnancy, I could feel Hedda around me. A lot. In fact, I had a dream after she passed away, and it was a very touching and intense dream. In that dream, she came to me because I had been missing her since her passing, and she hugged me. And I felt it. I could physically feel the pressure of her hug. She looked just like Hedda, but happy, and she was smiling. She told me how much I meant to her, and she gave me a hug. I was crying when I woke up, because I didn't want her to leave again. My husband woke up alarmed and asked me if anything was wrong, and I told him about the dream I had just had. But I didn't want to move out of that moment—I could still feel the love and the pressure of her hug. It was a really sweet moment. To this day, when I think about it, I can still feel it.

I gave birth to a beautiful boy we named Matthew. When I was in labor, somehow my thoughts wandered to Hedda, because I knew she was around. The doctors were very concerned because of my difficult pregnancy, and I had to have an emergency caesarean section, because, frankly, Matthew got stuck. I was never scared, though—I never questioned that he was going to be okay, and I felt that way because of Hedda. I just felt like between Hedda and my grandparents, nothing was going to happen to that baby. And nothing did. He was beautiful. And he still is. So are my other three children—triplets, all girls.

It was hard when Hedda passed. And I felt guilty that I couldn't be there, after having promised her that I would be. If I hadn't been on bed rest, if she hadn't developed shingles, I would have been there, and I would have been in charge of her care. I could have been there to hold her hand and tell her it was okay. After having such a close relationship with her, I worry about getting a little too close to patients, since their eventual passing causes such pain. I have had a lot of very nice relationships with patients since then, but I'm not as close to them as I had been to her. But they still need me—some won't sign their Do Not Resuscitate order unless I'm there with them, and some just want me to be around to tell them it's okay to let go when the time comes. So I still put all of my heart into my work, not in spite of a circumstance like Hedda, but because of it. They are as moved by what I have done for them as I am by what they have done for me. And we still work together—where they are uncomfortable talking about hospice care or their fear of dying, I'm comfortable enough with them to have that talk with them. If I can take some fear away from them, then they can pass away comfortably and with dignity. Patients sometimes need permission from people they trust in order to let go—just to tell them it's okay to let go takes a lot of courage and compassion. We're all born, we live, we eventually get sick, and we die. If I can make it easier with whatever tools I have, both medical and spiritual, then so be it. I have done not only my work, but my job as a human being in this lifetime.

THE SESSION

"Okay, so there is a female in the room so far. Family, yes, but not by blood. Make sense?"

"Yes."

"Well, yeah, of course it has to be somebody. Otherwise, why would she show up? That was a dumb thing for me to say. She knew she was going to pass on."

"Mmm-hmm."

"I see a uniform. Either something to do with a uniform or it is a symbol for work. So the *family* connection may be in the work sense. Yeah, I don't know why, but she tells me again she knew she was going to pass on."

"Mmm-hmm."

"There's the feeling that it was just a question of time. Actually— well, I'm sure everybody would be, so I shouldn't be so cynical— actually [she] admits she was kind of nervous about passing on."

"Yes."

"I don't mean to laugh, but she just made a joke—'If I had to do it all over again, I could do it blindfolded.'"

(Laughs) "Okay."

"She definitely has a nice sense of humor. Now . . . okay, I'm just going to state what I hear . . . [she] states she had bad health concerns. I mean, obviously something life threatening, because she says to me she passed from something health related."

"Okay, yes."

"But she said to me—bad. She might have survived for a time, but as she brings up, it's almost like when she was diagnosed she thought, *Who am I kidding?* I keep seeing the Certificate of Death in *The Wizard of Oz*—it's a sign to me that she thought, *I know I'm going to pass on, I'm going to try my best to get well, because there have been cases where people do get well . . .* and she does show me that she was doing okay for a while."

"Yes."

"She says it was like a roller coaster ride. It was going well, then it wasn't, then it was, and then it wasn't. But toward the end, she talks about passing in a sleep state. And she figured, *Okay, it's over.* As far as she's concerned—wanting to call a spade a spade—you fight for so long, and then when things start going downhill you start to give up, or give in. But she did put up a fight. I keep hearing that song *Put On a Happy Face,* so her attitude was positive and she was trying to keep everything upbeat. But she was actually glad to realize it was her time to pass. Because she says, if it wasn't, they would have sent her back. Or she would have gotten better, or whatever. One thing she learned is that you don't get there unless you're supposed to be there. Of course, again, she says that if somebody took their own life, well, that's different. Or, because she doesn't want any confusion, even if you knew you were going to pass on, and you were [trying] to speed up the inevitable, you're still supposed to be there. It's just a question of time. She blesses you for being good to her prior to her passing. She does state that you did calm her fears."

"Yes."

"She brings up about the emotional support being a big plus. She knows you're not conceited and won't take any credit for it, but she says the simplest things wind up being the most profound. She's also not going to bullshit you—she's glad it's over with."

(Laughs) "Okay."

"I don't know if this is correct, but they gave her some sort of treatment like chemo? See, I don't know if there's any other kind of treatment. So I don't know if she's showing me chemo to mean chemotherapy or just treatment."

"Yes."

". . . Because she admits always feeling nauseous from it. She shows me Pepto-Bismol, but tells me it wasn't as simple as that."

"Right."

"And she's not trying to sound like a martyr, but now that it's all over, she felt like she was being eaten from the inside out. One thing she says that still kind of amazes her is that she was sick and didn't know it. It's there doing its destruction . . . and she's young . . . so she was definitely surprised by the diagnosis. She goes in thinking it's going to be something else, and then by the time it's found, the damage is done. It amazes her that it was there all that time doing its damage, and she was going on with her life."

"Yes."

"But she definitely is taken aback by the diagnosis. And figured in the back of her mind that this was probably it. She certainly had a rough time prior to her passing, and a lot of it in silence. Actually, most of it in silence. She was thinking she was going to beat it, understood?"

"Yes."

"She says, 'Does it sound dumb to say this? I did beat it.'"

"Okay."

"It's just that there was a lot of suffering in silence. And as she states, we never think this, but at some point your body just can't take it anymore. And then it starts to affect you spiritually. She says that you just get beat to shit—physically, spiritually, emotionally— everything. Even to the point where the spirit—your soul—gets tired. Everything is fighting a losing battle. She says your body just gives out. But she does admit that when she first got there, she thought she was dreaming. Her passing was like walking from one room to the next—there's no public announcement. You just pass on. But she does tell me that even [though] she arrived okay, and joked that she could do it blindfolded, she did take a rest for a time when she got there. Because again, the spirit has been beat up also. She's kind of like, back and forth—she was a little on the fence about there being an afterlife?"

"I'm not sure. She said she believed."

"I guess the thing she wants to bring up is that as much as you want to believe, you just don't really know for sure until you know. She was probably more open-minded to it, rather than thinking you just die and that's the end of it. But she says to me that until you learn it for yourself, nobody really knows. Again, she was uncertain of exactly what was going to happen—she wasn't exactly expecting Saint Peter to meet her at the pearly gates. As much as you want to believe, she says you don't know until you know. Also, so this is clearly understood, she does thank you for helping to put her at ease. And that was a big help to her. You took care of her, she tells me, in more ways than one, but you also prepared her. She says you did soothe her and help ease her into it. She tells me she has come in dreams. You may not be sure, but she tells me she has visited."

"Right."

"She brings up her own family. So there must have been people here for her as well as there. She brings up her own family, but pulls me in both directions—over here and over there."

"I'm not sure."

"Okay, that's understandable—*family* is used very loosely by the souls, and it includes family by choice—friends, people who care, whatever. It's a term of endearment. But when she was here, she tells me she was kind of a lonely person."

"Yes."

"She admits to that. Not that she was a phony or anything, but she gives me the impression she was a good actress in hiding her feelings of loneliness. Again I hear *Put On a Happy Face*—because she puts up a front."

"Okay."

"I don't know how much you know about her personally, so don't say anything, but she's giving me the impression she'd kind of had it with everything here."

"Mmm-hmm."

"I kind of feel bad for her because she seems to have been a very lonely person. She's very sensitive, which is a blessing but can also be a curse. . . . She brings up again being very lonely, but it was just not something she wanted to talk about when she was here. Again she brings up family, but she brings up herself as family to you . . . you and she sort of became family. By term of endearment."

"Yes."

"I don't know how much you really know about her—she says she didn't have the easiest life here."

"Yes."

". . . Because she can't deny she's glad to be out of here. She's glad to be finished . . . I mean, you may know or you may not know, but she gives me the feeling that growing up she really didn't have anybody."

"Mmm-hmm."

"She does admit, and she's not putting this existence down, but she says she did have a lot of disappointment here. And she's giving me the feeling that some of this you may know, and some of it you may not know. But I guess because it's hard to believe, she admits that the feeling of being very alone did contribute to her health troubles. You know—now, keep in mind that they come to you in a manner that you know what they're talking about, so I'm not going to question anything, but she admits that loneliness is a contributing factor in her illness. But as she says, some people need their illness to receive love and affection. And some people need their illness in order to give love and affection. She's showing me a math equation—it's like two plus two equals four—she's come to realize there was a reason she was ill, there was a reason you were there, and that everybody played their role according to the equation. She says that if she hadn't become ill, you wouldn't have known her from Adam."

"Yes."

"Your paths would have had no reason to cross. You did what you were supposed to do. But she does recognize it was also very heartbreaking for you. It's tough to keep your emotions out of it. But she's certainly all right and in a happy place. And very pleased to say that. She says that one of the greatest struggles here is having feelings. Feelings can be a real troublemaker just as much as being something positive. She might not have expressed this to you, but she does admit she took it very personally when the illness was discovered. She doesn't want to sound like a crybaby, but she didn't have the easiest life here. And getting sick was just the icing on the cake. She was thinking, *Well, doesn't this just figure that this would happen to me.*"

"Yes."

"But she realizes now that there is a joyous ending to it. She says that it was all part of her life experience. I don't mean this in an unkind sense, but she was a bit of a good actress, yes?"

"Yes."

"I feel I'm not afraid to express myself, but also keeping my feelings to myself. She says she had to learn to trust. I don't know if you know anything about her upbringing, but I'm sensing a lack of trust in her environment growing up. It's like one day everything could be okay, and then the next day everything is in the toilet, so she doesn't trust anything. Nothing seems to be constant. None of her relationships was consistent in closeness. In her upbringing, and as a grown woman. But she was a fighter."

"Yes."

"It's funny—it's like her body was speaking to her. And it said at one point, *Just let me go, it's not getting any better.* And as she says, it's something we're all going to face sooner or later. You get to the point where you just think, *What's the use?* She had abandonment issues?"

"Could be, I'm not sure."

"It's like she has a family, but she doesn't have a family. Feelings of loneliness, isolation, not being able to trust—she says that we may see it that she had a very sad life, but she's come to understand it was a fulfilling life. She says we don't understand how valuable these moments were until we get to the hereafter, and you do your life review, and just like that math problem, everything fits in neatly. Her folks are passed, yes?"

"I don't really know."

"She brings her folks up, but it's so vague I can't tell if their death is in the physical or in the emotional sense. I don't want to say it, because I don't think it's true, but it almost feels like to me that she was adopted. Because she has parents, but they don't seem to be around, again either in the physical or emotional sense."

"I'm not sure, but nobody was there for her that I knew about."

"This is interesting—she brings up the subject of reincarnation. And she says she's not too eager about coming back any time soon."

(*Laughs*) "I understand."

"She's actually glad that it turned out to be even better than she had anticipated. Again, it's all part of her life experience. This is strange—there were people there for her, but nobody was around. She keeps showing me hot and cold water—that things keep changing. And brings up the aloneness issue. And she seemed to say earlier that she might have been apprehensive about passing on because she felt that nobody was going to be there for her. And she wasn't really sure who to expect there, either. At that point, she wasn't even sure if she wanted anybody to be there for her. So many hang-ups from here made her apprehensive of who she'd have to deal with in the hereafter. But it's interesting—she shows me animals, animals meeting her to put her at ease. They could have been her pets [who] passed on, or just animals in general. But they were there to ease the transition and bring her peace. It's almost the way they use animals for emotional and even physical therapy here."

"Right."

"Again, they put you at ease whether you know them or not. You never feel threatened by their presence. There must have been a lot of confusion with her upbringing. I don't know what to make of it either. She seems to feel trapped in her situation—and sad to hear this, but she just didn't feel loved here. It's heartbreaking to hear. Some people who could feel that way might not give a rat's ass, but she was sensitive, and it bothered her greatly."

"Yes."

"That's why they again state that in a situation like hers, the Divine Presence may send animals to ease her transition rather than people. It's less complicated and much less to have to worry about. It seems on the earth she was inclined to be a people-pleaser."

"Oh yes."

"And that's dangerous, given what she experienced. She shows me the good little Catholic schoolgirl's uniform—I don't know if she was, but it could be just my symbol to understand as one Catholic school kid to another. You're taught to be selfless, do everything right, and keep everybody happy. And if it doesn't happen, then you're just not trying hard enough."

"I understand."

"But once again, she brings up that she took her diagnosis and illness personally. Like a personal cheap shot. Like it was a page out of her past. It seems she blamed herself sometimes for things that went on here, even if they weren't within her control. And it's why she took the diagnosis so personally—it's like, just one more kick in the pants from the past. And not to be redundant, but again she states she's glad to be the hell out of here."

(*Laughs*) "Good."

"She's not feeling alone over there. She tells me she followed the animals to a place where she could rest. And that's exactly what she did. It's so that the feelings of loneliness and isolation from people here could wash away from her soul along with the physical illness that robbed her spirit. She understands now that all that trouble was part of her spiritual fulfillment, and that does add to her joyfulness in the hereafter. She realizes that she went through it all and made it to the finish line. All of that really made her radiate joy."

"Good."

"She said that near the end she was afraid of being afraid. But the transition was much easier than she expected. It kind of made up for a lot of the problems she faced here. She seemed unlucky in relationships—nothing seemed to work out—not lucky in love, that's for sure."

"No, not at all."

"Not to sound like a martyr, but often she feels like she was strung along. But she herself could be a bit of a loner as well. That was her safety zone. She shows me a net, like a net under a trapeze artist."

"Yes."

"But she certainly commends you for helping her have a happy ending. She gives you a lot of credit for something—before she passed away, she was glad that she was able to believe you were sincere in your friendship. Because she would be inclined not to trust people. But she trusted you. That little push helped her to get to the finish line, and to pass in peace. She's in a much better frame of mind over there. She mentions, however, that she was used here, in many ways."

"Yes."

"And that seems to be the thing that stuck in her side, even when she got to the hereafter. It was something she had to reconcile. She was a little naïve, and in her case it was dangerous. She came to realize that being used, though, was a bit her fault. She felt *stung* by it. As she understands now, she thinks perhaps she may have set herself up for some of the problems. And instead of throwing in the towel when she knew things were not working out, she fell back into the same routine of trying to please, trying to correct."

"Yes."

"She's also come to realize that it was okay to be alone, and there was no need to be frightened of it. We aren't conditioned to think that way, but it was actually okay, and there was no need to let the emotion of feeling lonely overwhelm her. She also realizes from over there that some people here found her to be a bit of a pain in the ass."

(*Laughs*) "Okay."

". . . But her heart is in the right place."

"Most definitely."

"And she's okay with having been seen that way. She says that even over on the other side—she doesn't want to give the impression that when you cross over, everything becomes fine. She says it's okay to go over there and still feel a little bugged that she was used. She's found her peace with it, but it's a process dealing with it before she can release it. She says she suffered here from a broken heart, but she came to realize that it was not necessary to do everything right here all the time. We're so conditioned here to think everything has to be done the way we're told it should be; otherwise, you're not doing it right. But she's learned over there that there is no *right*—it's what we do that makes sense within our soul, and that makes it the right thing to do. Even if it doesn't have the result we had hoped. She's learned now that it's okay to be sad, or to be depressed, regardless of the fact that we get conditioned here that we can't or *shouldn't* feel those things. She says you can't find yourself—here or hereafter—until you've experienced both the good and the bad. They are both necessary. But again, she appreciates your caring and compassion, because she knows you didn't have to do it."

"Well—I understand."

"She says let's be honest with each other—you didn't have to care as much as you did, or give as much as you gave. But it's your own women's intuition that sensed she needed that extra care—that extra shot in the arm. And it meant all the more to her, because, like she mentioned before, nobody else was there. There was no family, no friend. But then again, she says she comes to the understanding over there that she shouldn't have been too surprised nobody was there. But when it really mattered, she knew somebody *was* there for her. *You* were. You may have been a stranger to her in the bigger sense, but to her, at the time, and in her passing, you were family. And she considers herself very lucky to have had you."

"Thank you."

"She says she passes on young by today's standard."

"Yes."

"And even though she's a grown woman, she was still a little girl inside."

"Yes."

"She says she's made friends over there. She mentions a Susan, but I don't think it would be anybody you would recognize. She mentions making friends, and especially with souls who had also gone through lonely times or feeling sad and isolated on the earth. So that in itself is a huge triumph. I don't know if it's somebody trying to get my attention, but somebody calls out the name George."

"I'm not sure."

"It seems to be with her. But she's talking about making friends, so you're not going to know these people any more than I would. But these people have their heart in the same place as she does. They're on the same vibration and they understand each other. They are souls who were also not the happiest people on earth, but now they have triumphed. And again, says she has no intention of coming back any time soon."

(Laughs) "Okay."

"I hate to keep saying it, but again—I can't help but feel from her how sad she was."

"She was a very sad woman."

". . . It's why I'm so glad to hear she's all right, and in a happy, peaceful place, and in harmony with herself and others. She's dealing with the issues of being used and even making herself sick. It's funny—she says she just wanted to be loved."

"That's her."

"That's why, by the time this illness comes, she'd already had it. Hmm . . . that's nice to hear . . . the only thing she does regret is that she didn't meet you sooner."

"Aww."

"It wouldn't have happened right away, but your kindness would have helped her put her defenses down. But she says it was better to have known you at all than not to have met you. She thanks you for helping her find her way—she was a little girl who was lost, and your kindness helped her find her way. It's rather amazing that she let her defenses down with you. To a degree, she says."

"Mmm-hmm."

"Now, just in a general sense, because she seemed to have the most need to be heard—but she does bring up that there are other people over there that you did look after and look out for. She didn't know them, but she says there are other souls there, both male and female, who you kind of got ready. There's a male presence in the room who says exactly that—you got him ready. He says that everybody is going to get cold feet, so having a kind face and a friend to help ease the transition is wonderful. One thing your friend tells me to tell you is that you are in the right profession. You might have thought to yourself, *How did this come my way?* But it was supposed to. That's your life's work. And she says that you're spiritually supportive but you're not overwhelming or judgmental. You allowed them their dignity. She does genuinely feel like you loved her, at least for the time she knew you. So in that brief time she was able to experience that kind of love and sincerity. So she says, 'You crossed my path at exactly the right time.' Again, you were where you were supposed to be, and if she didn't get sick, she never would have known you.

They are telling me they are pulling back, but with an expression of gratitude. They realize that there is only so much you can do, and that's okay. Nobody was expecting miracles. But one thing she does want to emphasize is that you made an amazing emotional impression on her before she passed. And she knows you won't think it was any big deal. But it was. To them. And it's part of *your* learning experience—to accept praise. We've all been taught not to be prideful, but she says why shouldn't someone feel good about themselves in the fact that they made a big impression on somebody's life at the most important time in their life—before they left the earth. When you think about it, what's wrong with that? She extends white roses to you from over there, spiritually.

And she's starting to pull back with the rest. But she's sincerely glad to tell you she's all right and in a happy place. I would say she deserves it."

"Oh yes, she does."

"And she has also come to realize there that she does deserve it."

"Good."

"She says the souls have told her, and she's come to realize it on her own that she's earned her peace and joy. With that she pulls back with the others, and expresses her gratitude until she sees you again, because she knows your paths will cross again one day, just as [they] did here. She'll be with you to reciprocate your kindness when it's your time to pass, so that you feel safe, happy, and not afraid. And with that, they go."

I love stories like these, probably because they happen with a greater frequency than people realize. As well as we may know somebody, we may not ever know the impact our love, caring, and compassion may have had on their life. Until under some lucky circumstance they are able to come back after the fact and tell us. Sometimes a soul will come through who is not significant enough to immediately spring to the sitter's mind, but when the soul presses them and reminds them about even the briefest of circumstances, they start to remember. Sometimes the circumstance of their meeting was very short, but it made an impact on that soul, who never forgot the kindness they received and thought enough of it to want to appear in a session to remind them, and to thank them for it.

I remember a session with Andrew during which he racked his brain trying to remember a woman named Goldy, who had wandered into his session near the end. Just when I was ready to give up, she said, "perfume," and all the lights went on for Andrew. "Yes," he said, "but we only worked together for one day." He remembered working a post-college job as a fragrance model in Bloomingdale's. During a store promotion, a coworker who was much older than the rest of the twentysomething models was having a hard time keeping up with the demands of the job. Andrew teamed up with her to help her make some sales—in reality, so she wouldn't be fired. At the end of the day, she thanked him, but never came back. In the session, she explained to both of us that that one day restored her faith in the kindness of people. She was recently widowed, alone, scared, and having to make her way in the world again. She thanked Andrew for his kindness, even if it was only one day, and told him how much it had meant to her that he spent the time with her.

We never know how our actions, good and bad, will affect another person. But anything that is done in kindness is never forgotten by the souls, or by the Infinite Light. It's like a savings account—all the good goes in and waits for us, all the while gaining interest and building with the other kindnesses, until they all redeem themselves for us in the world hereafter. People can tell me, sometimes with startling detail, some of the terrible things they have done on the earth, but nobody seems to remember the kind things they did. I suppose it is a real sign of our humanity that we don't keep count of every time we are nice to somebody, but not to recall them at all seems sad to me. We may not remember, but the people to whom the kindness was done will never forget. They bring it with them like a gift to the hereafter, and they take that gift and shower us with it and more, to thank us for being special to them when they needed it most. It's something to remember—not just the lesson, but the kindness. Remember it if you can, but don't fret if you can't. Trust me, somebody will.

8

YOU ARE HERE

MICHAEL

There is a Zen proverb I love: "Let go or be dragged." This one statement crystallizes beautifully what the souls try to teach us about letting the journey of our lives take its twists and turns, and to trust that the outcome will be exactly what is was supposed to be. Some of us start to get concerned when the path isn't as clear as we thought it would be. Many of us start to panic when the direction doesn't always seem certain. But the souls have made it evident that sometimes, in some journeys, we will walk on our path, only to be blown into another portal, another circumstance, that forces us to rethink everything we have learned up to that point. We may go kicking and screaming, but it is where we have to go. It is where we were meant to be. I think no story illustrates this concept as well as the unlikely life of Michael.

Truth be told, my memory isn't the greatest. After having met with tens of thousands of clients over the last four decades, I just can't remember all the names, faces, and details from all my sessions. Yet when I recently met Sally Darrow, Michael's mom, I somehow got it into my head that the soul of a crazy redhead would make herself known. I don't know why. In her session, her brother, who had taken his life some months before, made an appearance. But during the session, a funny thing happened—the crazy redhead showed up! All at once, Sally's story came back to me.

Sally had originally visited me years ago when she lost a son to suicide. He was only fourteen years old. I remember thinking at the time that this couldn't be possible, because Sally didn't even look old enough to have children. Moreover, she attended the session with her mom, and I assumed the boy calling out to her as *Mom* during the session was the son of the woman with Sally. After he told me to just listen to him and not make assumptions, *she* appeared: the crazy redhead I somehow remembered. I knew her from before, I just felt it, and this jovial, funny woman told me she was Sally's sister, and yes, I had met her before. My heart started to feel heavy—I thought, *Holy cow, how many people did this woman lose?* How does a woman with that much loss and devastation come into a room, smiling, outgoing, charming, and not be a total mess? To know Sally is to know how incredible a person she is, and then it's an easy question to answer. She's Sally, and *somebody* has to be.

After the session, Sally told me she had originally come to see me with her mom shortly after her sister took her life, and I remembered having so much fun communicating with this fiery redhead who was irreverent and funny, smart, and good-hearted. I even remembered thinking at the time that it must have been a terrible blow to lose a sister who had such *life*. But her sister acknowledged that she had problems on the earth, and that sometimes, mental turmoil can be as fatal as terminal cancer. I remembered why I liked her so much, and I remembered why Sally was such a wonderful person.

I'm sorry to say that Sally's life has made her a bit of a steady customer. I wouldn't wish that kind of grief and heartache on another living soul. But she carries it, and in spite of it, she continues in a way that has made me proud. But something strange happened during her last session after her brother had passed: I was communicating with the usual—and now fairly familiar—cast of characters, when a little girl appeared, seemingly no one from Sally's life. It was clear to me she wasn't a relative, and she didn't even feel like a friend or associate. Just a little girl who wanted to say hello. For a minute I thought she may have wandered into the wrong session, but she talked to Sally like she knew her, and then referenced Sally's son Michael.

They had no idea who this little girl was, and I was not at all able to help them out. But she had a message for Michael—she said she was watching him and helping him the best she could, but that he also had to help himself. Then, in an instant, all the lights went on for Sally, and she sat in awe of what she heard.

Some months later, Sally confided in us that the message was indeed for Michael. He was a surviving veteran of the war in Iraq, dealing with PTSD, and trying to stay clean and sober after drug and alcohol addiction. She told us that when Michael heard the recording of her session that included the little girl, he cried. He cried and was worried. Now he knew people were watching him, and that his struggle to stay clean and sober was not just his own. As much as the message from the little girl touched him, it also unnerved him. He knew he could lie to himself, his mother, and his friends about sobriety, but he couldn't lie to the souls. So the message was both an encouragement and a warning. We were intrigued to hear about this odd turn of events in her session, so we asked Sally if her son was amenable to sitting for a session. We were curious about what else the souls could tell him, and if the little girl was just an anomaly or if she really was part of his growth here and his support system from the hereafter.

I have nephews in the armed forces. I know firsthand the dangers and pitfalls of military life, especially during and after combat. So if the session with Michael could be just one more arrow in his quiver of wellness and peace, then it was a good idea all around. Though Michael said yes, and the hour of communication turned out to be something more touching, inspirational, and poignant than many sessions I can remember, he asked his mom, Sally, to tell his story. He was just unable to relive the horror he experienced as a soldier. We honored Michael's request. His session with us then follows.

This is Sally's story about Michael, in her own words:

Michael was born in February 1986. I was always going to name him Michael, and when he was born, I looked at him, and he had red hair. My mom was there and she laughed. "A redheaded Michael," she said, and I asked her what that was supposed to mean, and she just laughed and said, "You'll see, honey, you'll see." And I found out what she meant. He was the most joyful out of all my four kids; he was the most loving and loved being around people. He loved being the center of attention, but wasn't the kind of kid who *had* to be the center of attention and just got on people's nerves. People loved to be with him, and he was so happy. But underneath all this joy and happiness, I could always detect a little bit of sadness about him. It was something I couldn't really pinpoint until I grew up a little bit. I was only nineteen when I had him, so

I didn't have a lot of life experience really. But I could detect some bit of sadness. I didn't really know what that was until I got more experienced as a mom.

Two years later, I had another son. Michael was a little Mommy's helper for me at that point, and was really good with his little brother. At five or six years old, Michael wanted to be around the adults. He was funny, and he would round up all his cousins because we had a close family, and Michael would always be their leader. He always wound up being front and center of everything. He had these big, beautiful green-blue eyes and this red hair. Not a carrot top, but beautiful red hair, and a huge smile always. He was a joy, and he always made me smile. Even when he got into mischief, like coming in the house covered with mud from head to toe, I couldn't even get mad at him, because all he would do is giggle and look sheepish, and just make me laugh. He was the kid that everybody noticed, just happy-go-lucky, always smiling and surrounded by friends.

Michael wanted everybody to be happy all the time because *he* felt happy all the time. He didn't understand anything having to do with sadness. I think whatever sadness I saw in him was because he knew people around him sometimes couldn't be happy all the time. This became especially true when his dad and I got divorced. From that point on, going back and forth between me and his dad, you could see it in his eyes. No matter how much he was smiling, or laughing his contagious laugh, you could see a certain dimness in his eyes. He didn't understand why we couldn't be a happy family, why we couldn't all live together anymore. I take full responsibility for that sadness in him. The lights went out a little bit in him. He was happy all the time, but he knew his mom and dad were not together anymore. Sometimes, he would cry, and he had never cried before. The smile was still there, but the smile in his eyes was never as bright again.

In school, Michael was Mr. Popularity. He played basketball, he played football, he played baseball—anything he could get involved with, he did. He loved his friends and had tons of them, and he was a very good student. He was always excited to share his good grades, from math to art. He was good at all of it, and found great joy in all of it. Michael did not know what it was like to be a gossip or a bully, or even to bicker with friends—the usual teenage stuff. He never experienced it, nor did he ever feel the need to fight with, bully, or even say a bad word about anybody else. He was the guy everybody wanted to be around.

In his freshman year of high school, he lettered on the golf team, and found that he had a natural gift with a golf club. But he became obsessed with the golf course, which became a little aggravating for me as a parent. Now that I look back, it was probably the first time I noticed the signs of an addictive personality, without even realizing it. Golf just became a little too important to him: not shooting a good number would leave him miserable, but doing a great job would make him elated for days. He could have gone pro. That was his dream, had circumstances not changed life for him—and all of us, really—forever. When Michael was sixteen years old, his fourteen-year-old brother Justin committed suicide by shooting himself in our home.

All of us, including Michael, lived in a state of shock for a long time. We didn't expect it, we didn't see the warnings—at all. Even looking back all these years later, it's really hard to see in Justin the typical signs of someone contemplating suicide. He just didn't have any. I think Michael may have taken it the worst of my children because he felt responsible. Michael had already moved in with me full-time, but Justin was still at his dad's house, and still going back and forth between us on different weeks. I think Michael felt he should have picked up more on any changes in Justin, or told me if there was anything he knew about that I should have known about, too. But he was sixteen years old, and he was doing what sixteen-year-old boys do—worrying about school, friends, and girls.

It happened on Halloween. And it changed Michael. It changed my eight-year-old daughter and my four-year-old son. It changed all of us. Forever. They are all different people today because of that tragedy. I can pinpoint the absolute 100 percent change in Michael from Halloween of 2002, when I lost him, too. I lost two boys that day. Justin, through death, and Michael, through life.

Michael just checked out after that. There was no more smile, there was some self-destructive behavior, there was blame, there was anger, and the big question he would keep asking was *Why not me?* And watching this was so difficult for me. I realize all these years later how little I mourned Justin's death because I was so consumed with trying to save Michael. I'm not angry about it, but I do realize it. As a parent you have to make choices and put out the fires that are in front of you, and I tried. Michael started disregarding curfew, checked out of school (though he did finish his education online), and started drinking. He didn't feel like he deserved to be happy because his brother had died and he hadn't. He was smoking pot and drinking to excess, and it was traumatizing, especially his "I don't care anymore" attitude. But he did reach out for help, and he asked to be checked into a mental health facility. He started peer counseling, and he started doing well. He was also surprised to find a number of Justin's friends there, who had also been affected by Justin's suicide. He was there for a month, and then for a while would go in and out when the self-destructive behavior returned. But when he was there, and straight, he was a leader—he would be the group leader and the one the other kids would listen to, and he was loved by the counselors and doctors, and even the other kids' parents. So when he was on, he stayed on, but when he fell off, he knew what was wrong and tried to pull it back together. He still battled the question of why it was his brother who had died and not him. It just seemed to be something nobody could answer for him.

Ever since Michael was a little kid, he wanted to join the army. Justin wanted to go into the air force, and Michael wanted to be G.I. Joe. Michael got sober after some time at the facility, and he thought going into the army would give him some structure in his life and help kick-start his education through the G.I. Bill. It was the one thing he could follow through on that he and Justin had planned together. He was determined to do it, and he got himself sober and healthy. He believed at the time, after September 11, 2001, that it was something he needed to do—not just for Justin, but because it was something he had set his mind on years ago, and because he wanted to make something out of himself. I think the proudest moment of my life was watching him graduate from basic training—to watch one of those ceremonies is breathtaking. Michael had such pride in himself, and confidence that he hadn't felt since he was on a golf course. He challenged himself and he won. He finally was at the top of his game, and people were in awe of him, including his commanders.

Michael was deployed to Iraq in October 2006. He was in the middle of his deployment during the Iraq War troop surge, where

George Bush sent an additional twenty thousand troops to the area, and extended the tours of the troops already there. It was the bloodiest part of the war. Michael absolutely did not think he would make it back from that deployment. I don't think any of the people he was with did. Soldiers were dying around him, getting limbs blown off, and again he started thinking, *Why not me?* And the more it didn't happen to him, the worse it got for him. He was suffering a lot of survivor's guilt. He did have his share of mishaps and near misses—being blown out of a Humvee and suffering a blast concussion, getting hit on the head with falling concrete—he suffered a few head injuries there. But he still did things that were up front, out front, where if it *was* going to be him, it would have been. He was fearless that way. He knew if he was going to go down, then he was going to go down a hero.

His unit was assigned to guard a school of Iraqi children, because insurgents were killing their own people. The insurgents were no more than kids themselves—sixteen or seventeen years old—but this was also a war between the Sunni minority that had been governing the Shiite majority for years, and were now losing power. So in addition to killing Americans, insurgents—basically street thugs—were killing their own people, including children. So the American soldiers were the good guys to the Shiites, helping to keep them safe. And the children loved them. Children seem to naturally gravitate to Michael, but these children *flocked* around him, especially one little girl, who Michael became quite fond of, and she of him. She developed a little crush on him, and called him *mah soldier*. They got to know the children very well, and would often give them little gifts or bring them candy when they could get it in a care package from home.

On Christmas day, Michael was posing for a picture with the

children, to send home after telling us so much about them. The little girl asked to be in a picture with Michael, and he dropped to one knee with his arm around her and smiled. Gunshots started ringing out from the insurgents, killing the little girl under his arm. They started spraying bullets all over the schoolyard, killing the running children. Children with *Dora the Explorer* backpacks and coloring books. And as quickly as it had started, the bloodshed was over. And again, Michael drove himself crazy thinking it should have been him, not her. Not her. She was just a little girl.

I got a call from him sometime after the firefight. The chaplain had him call me to help him connect with people he loved, and bring him back to reality after the trauma of what he had witnessed. I remember that he literally made no sense on the phone. He was speaking so fast, and rambling, and I was really worried for his sanity. I was relieved to know he was okay physically, but it was clear he was devastated by what he saw. War is war, but these were *children*. I didn't fully understand his devastation until I got a package from him, and in it were haunting pictures of the kids in the weeks before, with their big smiles, and his beloved little girl, posing and smiling for the camera.

Michael's deployment was finished in December 2008. When he came home, he had already reenlisted for another deployment. He wanted to go back—he wanted to stay in the army. He wanted to move up in the ranks and at least try to make a difference in a place like Iraq. He wanted to be part of the nation-building, after the inhumanity that he had seen there. He started training to get into a special unit, but he wound up blowing out his knee. And then he was out. He could not go back. And it was just as well. He was so different—*altered*. Although many veterans have difficulty showing emotion, Michael was able to. I don't know how he was with other people, but with his mom he could let go. He could cry, he could explain, and he could express what he was feeling. But it did not stop him from drinking again. He thought things were getting back to normal, but I knew he was far from it. He started experiencing headaches, confusion, and seizures. He would call me, and he wasn't talking in normal sentences or making sense, but he thought he was. On the base, they checked him out and decided he was okay, but he wasn't. There were also physical changes in him—he would lose his balance, and he would have to tie his keys and his wallet to his pants so he wouldn't lose them. After complaining of the problems he was having, the doctors on the base started prescribing medications: medication to calm down, medication to sleep, medication to wake up, medication for pain—he was becoming so overmedicated that his personality changed as well. He was short with people, angry, then went from one spectrum of emotion to the other. Happy to sad, angry to laughing, hopeful to despondent. All in a short time. He was twenty-two years old and starting to get addicted to the narcotics, and there was really no medical oversight for him or many of the returning veterans who had experienced both emotional and physical trauma.

What I always find comical in this tragedy is that Michael developed a heroin dependency for basically one reason—because he didn't like the way the pills made him feel. Or the alcohol. People didn't want to be around him when he was like that, so he tried to find a different way to numb the pain. Heroin had become an epidemic in most of the small Midwestern towns in the U.S., including ours, so it was everywhere and easy to get. He started by snorting it, and then began injecting it. I knew something wasn't right with him—he was thin, and he would fall asleep standing up. I didn't ever want to think my kid was using heroin. That he would ever put a needle in his arm. But then the spoons began going missing from my kitchen. I found the orange caps that go on the syringes. That was what got me to wake up and realize that if we didn't do something, he was going to die. We decided to check him into a VA mental health facility.

Michael did great. He really engaged in the therapy and was being given opiate blockers. He understood that he wasn't alone, that he wasn't crazy, and that he wasn't the only one going through this. He started to understand that PTSD was a very real and very dangerous thing. He worked really hard, but the screaming and the crying he heard so much in Iraq still echoed in his ears, and he couldn't escape it. He transferred to the Warrior Transition Unit at the hospital, but again, the main protocol was to medicate them and often misdiagnose them, and some veterans were not surviving the treatment. This is only a mother's opinion, but I feel like the Veteran's Administration was failing so many of these veterans—they were just not getting the help and the support they desperately needed.

Michael got out eventually, but he wasn't ready. He tried to go out with his friends, and he tried to be normal, but he wasn't ready. He did things excessively—drink, buy a lot of clothes, spent money like water—and he lived like there was no future for him. No matter how many lives he had saved in Iraq, he still didn't feel like he deserved to live. He never acknowledged the positive things he had done—only what he had failed at. He started using again. And I begged him to stay alive. He had lived through a war, and I didn't want to lose him to drugs now that he was home. I told him I couldn't lose another child, and he swore to me that he wasn't trying to kill himself. But heroin is the devil. When you use it, you feel *nothing*. You don't feel about anything, you don't care about anything. You just want to stop the hurt. While the prescription medications made him feel sleepy or drugged all the time, the heroin made him feel nothing.

One day Michael was out of money for his drugs. There was a woman on the street who had forty dollars in her hand, and Michael snatched it from her. As soon as he did it, he stopped and threw the money on the ground, telling her *I'm sorry, I'm so sorry*, and ran away. But he dropped his cell phone, so they knew who he was. He called me to tell me, and I met him over at the VA hospital. But I called the police. I knew that if I didn't hold him responsible that I was going to lose him. The woman he grabbed the money from didn't want to press charges when she heard he was a veteran, but he was arrested and brought to jail. This was his rock bottom—he was so ashamed of himself and he took responsibility for himself. He had many people, including doctors and military brass, who stood up for him in court, and he was given probation because the woman whose money he stole would not press charges. But after another slip, he appeared again in front of the judge and asked to spend the rest of his probation in jail in order to save his life. He started reading the Bible, started getting straight, and started getting sober. Things started to make sense to him more, and he started to accept that maybe God had a plan for him, and it was not to die.

What Michael wants most in the world is to one day run his own rehabilitation facility. For veterans, for drug users, for teenagers at risk, all based on what he has lived through. He wants to be able to tell people, *Your parents got divorced? So did mine. Check. You lost a sibling? So did I, I've been there. Check. You watched people die? So did I. Check.* He said that he had an epiphany that everything always leads to another, depending on how you look at it. He's had a lot of loss, and he could not understand it. But now he's beginning to understand that his losses were an education, and that he's not alone here. He struggled before with the concept of life in the hereafter, but now he knows they are watching him, helping him, and holding him accountable for more than just himself. He knows that people love and care for him. He's really trying to become independent now, and he knows that only Michael can fix him. He may not be completely fixed ever, but he can be successful in his life. Instead of asking, *Why not me?*, he's starting to understand his place on the earth and his job in this life. He can be a voice for all the people—his brother, his brothers in battle, the veterans still struggling, and the little girl—all the people who have passed before him. He can be *their* voice. It will forever be a day at a time, but he wants his life. He just wants to live.

THE SESSION

"Okay, so let's begin and see what happens. Let's see who comes to visit. Immediately, two males come forward. Now some other males also come forward, in a little group. Don't explain. There are some females also. And if you can, acknowledge out loud, because the souls seem to take off on the sound of your voice. I guess it's some kind of vibe they respond to."

"All right."

"One male comes forward in a fatherly manner, understood? He states he's dad, so I take it your dad has passed?"

"No."

"Then who is this man coming to you as Dad? Okay, don't explain. I could have made a mistake, and he could be calling out to your dad, and I misunderstood, thinking he is your dad. He comes in a fatherly manner, but must be on your father's side, because he keeps bringing up *dad* to me. So he's got to be a granddad or something, whether you expected him or not. And he brings your dad up."

"Okay."

"Since you told me your dad is still here, then it's apparent he's calling out to him. It's why when he stated *dad* I assumed he was your dad, passed on. Without any alarm, and don't read between the lines, but he does express health concern with your father. I'm not trying to be a wise guy, because nobody is getting any younger, but he tells him to keep alert, and to watch where he is walking, descending steps . . ."

"Yes."

". . . I get the impression you're not being told anything you don't already know. But he does express concern to be careful, descending stairs with him, whether it be in public or at home. Obviously some discomfort can be avoided, otherwise they wouldn't say anything. This also happened in the beginning, but I didn't know what to do with it, but I better open my mouth. There's a few men here, and let me just explain quickly—*family* is used very lightly there—it could be people through blood or marriage, and even by choice. Because there are some males here in the room, and they seem to have passed young, and look to me like they are in military uniform."

"Yes."

"And they bring up that they passed on in the war. What war

they mean, don't help me. I don't know. It could be the Crimean War, for all I know. But they talk about passing on in the war, and I just want to bring to your attention also that when they reach out, they do come to you in a manner assuming you know what they are talking about. So without helping me, as long as you acknowledge it, that's all we need. But there's at least two, maybe three."

"Yes."

"Definitely in uniform. I'll be honest with you, it looks militaristic to me. They aren't fireman."

"Okay, yes."

"They come around you as brothers. I keep seeing that television show *Band of Brothers*. They're not your real brothers, but a term of endearment. They know if they showed me *Band of Brothers* you'd know what they are trying to say."

"Yes."

"They give me the impression you've had a lot of tragedy in your life."

"Yes."

"They do express genuine concern toward you, and they don't mean this to be insensitive, but they tell me you're a mess. Understood?"

"Yes."

"They are around you kind of like brotherly guardian angels. They said to me you're a mess, but they did also compliment you, though, in being a survivor. They tell me you're a very sensitive guy—a very good trait, but it can also be trouble. They put a big ice cube over your head and press it down, and tell me to tell you that you have to try to cool down. They're doing it in a very nurturing, soothing manner. From what they tell me, I take it there must have been a period or time when you knew them in the military."

"Yes."

"So I'm assuming you were in the military at one time. They seem genuinely concerned about you oppressing yourself with guilt and remorse, and . . . not that they're not happy and in a good place over there, but one of them especially is a little frustrated in the fact that you may feel like you're here and they're not. But they say they're where they're supposed to be. Just like you are where you're supposed to be. You are here. If you were supposed to have passed on, it would have happened. But apparently, according to them—whether you believe this or not—it's not your time to be there. They seem like pretty *tell it like it is* type of guys. And they state not to do that to yourself—feeling a sense of guilt over their passing—because you're just not supposed to be there yet. One of them kind of jokes with you, 'What's so hard to understand?' Naturally, one of these days, as we all know, you're going to head that way. And when you're supposed to head that way, you'll go that way. But they do certainly tell me they are around you like guardian angels to help you to help yourself, but . . . even in your life presently, they tell me it's been a rocky road. I don't think I'd want to trade places with you, let me put it to you that way. But as they state, you still have to pat yourself on the back that efforts put forth have been rewarded—you're a survivor. You've probably been through things I couldn't even imagine happening to anybody, and that's why they say, 'What's wrong with feeling good about yourself?' You've gone through your experience, and there have been some falls and difficulties, but you're still moving forward. One of them over there jokes about being around you like a guardian angel, but teases you that they don't get paid overtime at the executive level."

(He laughs.)

"And that's why they say to cut yourself a break. From their perspective over there, everything is quite simple here. Unfortunately, people screw things up."

"Yes."

"Don't say anything. There's another male—another younger male. He comes as a brother."

"Yes."

"Okay, they are giving me the recycle symbol. That means start again because I skipped over something. Another male. The other males that were here in uniform—they're term-of-endearment brothers. But another male comes through, and he tells me he's the son-slash-brother passed on. But in this case he is actually your brother."

"Yes."

"He also speaks of a tragic passing. In the sense of his age of course, because he does tell me he passes over young, but circumstances also."

"Yes."

"He wants to make sure you understand you didn't fail him."

"Okay."

"I see that statue at Rockefeller Center in New York City, of Atlas holding up the world. And your brothers in the *Band of Brothers*, and your brother—they kind of complain to you that too many times you feel like Atlas holding up the world, and that's not how it's supposed to be."

"Yes."

"That's why your brother said to you, you couldn't save him. There was nothing you could do. One thing he states is that everybody here is in the driver's seat—everybody is responsible for their own lives and their own actions. And just because it doesn't turn out the way you feel it should, that doesn't mean that everything's all screwed up. Another thing . . . your brother does tell me you're a mess."

(He laughs.) "Yeah."

"Like your other brothers in the military did. If anything, they do complain to you that sometimes trying to get through to you is like trying to get a camel through the eye of a needle. And even your brother warns you—because he was in the same boat—very sensitive guy, great trait, but it can be a real troublemaker."

"Yes."

"Your brother tells me to tell you that he is all right and in a happy place. And as long as you know that, it will take some of the edge off. He hopes. The thing is, it does seem you're not only brothers, but good pals."

"Yes, for sure."

"But he does admit to me he could be a pain in the ass, too."

(Laughs) "Yes."

"That's normal—nobody's perfect. But the thing is, you're no holy roller, but he does thank you that you pray for him in your own way. And it's singularly private between you and he."

"Right."

"Neither of you is the mushy type, but he knows you love him and he loves you. And when you pray for him in your own way, it comes to him like a gift in the mail. He does admit he wasn't the happiest person here."

"Yeah."

"He's not going to give me a line of bull—he tells me he's kind of glad to be out of here. At the time of his passing . . . your folks are still on the earth? He calls out to your parents."

"Yes."

"I just got kind of yelled at over there because I put it in the form of a question. But he spoke about your parents, and he calls out to your parents. I know your dad is here—that's been covered. But he calls out to your mom and dad, and again states to them that he's all right and in a happy, safe place. He admits he had terrible anxiety here. And he tells me you know exactly what he is talking about."

"Yes."

"He talks about going through terrible anxieties and depression here."

"Yes."

"And again, you can fall into that pit also, at times. He's told me this a few times, so I have to assume I'm thinking the right way. He did tell me he contributed to ending his own life."

"Yes."

"But I don't like to use the S-word. His death certificate can say that, but so what—it's only a piece of paper. But the thing is, nobody really knows what kind of nightmares can be going on in someone's mind. He does tell me that at the time, he wasn't in the right frame of mind and that he can't be held responsible for your actions. Okay, he realizes now it wasn't a smart thing to do, but he was *sick at heart*."

"Yes."

"So I would say he passed from an illness. I strongly believe that if you're overwhelmed with depression and anxiety, can it kill you? You're damn right it can. They are illnesses. It can be too overwhelming for people, and that's what happened. Even over there, he admits that when he arrived—and there seems to be a part of him that didn't really believe there was a hereafter—but he states that they took him to a place of rest there, because as much as this was affecting him emotionally, physically, and mentally, it's also like jarring your nervous system, and affecting the soul as well. One thing he does bring up to you—you've had your thoughts about it also."

"Yes."

"And as your brother states—no good. You've progressed tremendously. And not everybody can do it. So don't feel conceited with yourself if you pat yourself on the back and keep moving. This is somebody who has gone into the wrong frame of mind, and what's happened has happened. But since he's been through that experience, he impresses you to—it's just that life in many ways has kicked you in the pants."

"Yes."

"And yet he insists that you're letting it overwhelm you because you're not looking at the fact that you are courageously surviving. Without telling me, you must have been through some rough stages."

"Yes."

"He's very proud of the fact that you're a survivor. And there was a time there where you were kind of on the edge."

"Yes, for sure."

"But I still see you going up the ladder. Efforts put forth have been rewarded. Everything didn't happen in one day—it's been steps and stages. But he's very proud of the fact that you've made tremendous progress. Also . . . there's talk of another brother . . . oh, but he states he's an uncle. So I have to assume one of your folks lost a brother. And this is why in the beginning I was afraid I was maybe doing something wrong. But I realize there were two males coming through as *brother*, but I'm glad your brother told me that he was the actual brother. He says the same thing—you have to get rid of that Atlas attitude. You're holding up the world. He says a lot of the emotions you hold on to is like walking around with the world on your back, and all it does is weigh you down. Also, too, and don't explain it . . . there's also a young female presence around you. Without saying anything . . . and the feeling of her passing on young. She reaches out to you as a daughter, but in the term-of-endearment sense."

"Okay."

"It's not your daughter, but I'm not going to give her an argument if that's how she wants to feel toward you. And also, too, it helps me because she's giving herself some sort of identity. Now, without telling me, she says you know who it is."

"Yes."

"She is another individual who is around you a lot, like a guardian angel. She does tell me that you and she had gone through a tough time together. At times—and she means this with love—at times even she gets a little frustrated with you, because you're carrying her passing on your shoulders."

"Yes."

"She says you have a lot on your plate. And she says you haven't seen it yet, because you're not there yet, but when your time comes and you're supposed to be there, you're going to come to the realization that although so many things in your life were terrible, you're going to see that you made it to the finish line. She does bless you from over there . . . in many ways you did in a sense save her life."

"Yes."

"And that's why she comes to you like your little adopted daughter, so to speak."

(Crying) "Okay."

"Whatever happened to her—how she passed—she sees it from over there as very par for the course. And the same thing—if she wasn't supposed to have passed on, she wouldn't be there. Actually . . . and this is very nice to hear . . . not that she's begrudging her existence on the earth, but as she states, you did save her from here."

"Yes."

"She says to me that she's all right, at peace, and in a happy, safe, peaceful place, but didn't have the easiest life on the earth. And certainly tells me that she didn't have any of the opportunities that might be afforded to children her age in the U.S."

"Yes."

"But she says loud and clear that you cannot hold yourself responsible or blame yourself for her passing. Prior to her passing, you must have been a tremendous joy in her life, and she in yours as well."

"Yes."

"You became like best pals."

"Yes."

"And like whatever you've gone through in the past few years, it's just rocked your boat to the point that sometimes you don't know whether you are coming or going."

"Yes."

"And as she states, stop putting yourself in the wrong frame of thinking. She says all of this is part of a unique experience. In a lot of ways you'll feel like you failed her, but as she and your brother say, there's no such thing—it doesn't exist. It's not failure, it's experience. You need to change the word, because that's what it is. Even though it's not a happy experience . . . as she says, your life for a time ran parallel with hers, which helped her to fulfill whatever her experience was supposed to be here. On a bad day, you may say, 'That sounds like a load of horse shit to me,' but as she says, you need to ask yourself, whose life is it anyway?"

(He laughs.) "Yes."

"In the short time she was here, she definitely gives me the impression she experienced so many things that it was really overwhelming for somebody her age."

"Yeah."

"But the same thing—she realizes now that it all fell into place. When she was on the earth, she might not have seen it that way. But over there, it all unfolds for her, and don't take this the wrong way, but she's kind of glad to be out of here."

"Yeah."

"She says the most frustrating thing, when they look into this dimension, is all the needless bull that goes on. Every day. She, your buddies over there, your brother and uncle—they actually feel sorry for us, because we're in the proving ground. This is Purgatory. Yet once you fulfill your purpose, you get to move on ahead. And . . . your little daughter, I'm going to call her . . . she doesn't hold anything against anybody with regard to her passing. She's making it like par for the course, like, what else could have possibly been expected?"

"Uh-huh."

"But the thing is, she states she's really all right and in a happy place. And she's also proud of herself that she got through her experience. Even though it didn't have a happy conclusion. But she says that's water under the bridge now—it's over with. And she's out of here."

"Good."

"But you certainly played a unique role in her life for the time that you did, for whatever reason. And she kind of breaks your chops in a nice way because you won't give yourself that credit. You're looking too much at the ugliness of everything."

"Yeah."

"She says that when she got there, she admits there was a trauma with her passing, and she didn't know what to make of it. At first she thought it was kind of a dream, but when she did her life review and everything fell into place, it only looked beautiful—there was no ugliness to it. There was purpose and fulfillment to everything she lived through. She doesn't expect us to see it that way, because we're conditioned to think of things how they are here. There's also . . . I don't want these people to think I'm ignoring them, but there are people around you who claim to be grandparents. So I'll speculate that the ones who have passed are reaching out to you."

"Okay."

"There's also talk of loss of a sister, but she claims she's an aunt."

"Yes."

"So I'm going to assume one of your folks lost a sister. She's there as well. Needless to say—but they say it anyway—there's been a tremendous amount of tragedy in your life."

"Yes."

"There's been a lot of deaths, sadnesses—pretty hairy ones. As your buddies kid with you, it's kind of *blanked* you up."

"Mmm-hmm."

"And yet, they feel—all of them—look at the fact that you're making tremendous recovery. And in your recovery, so much of what you have gone through is turning out—they feel—to be a blessing in disguise. Because not only will you help yourself, but also others as well. And in order to help, you had to have gone through it. Otherwise you're talking out of your *rear end*."

"Yes."

"Your aunt says that only another individual who [has] lost a child is going to understand how it feels to lose a child."

"Right."

"Like, my mother never lost a child. She would know somebody feels something, but she'd never be able to fully understand what they feel. Also, too—your people over there, and that includes your 'band of brothers,' your actual brother, your little daughter, I'll call her, your uncle, aunt, grandparents—they all say that what you've gone through has definitely screwed you up, because they tell me you did kind of fall into substance troubles, understood?"

"Yes."

"You have to cut yourself some slack on that. But you're recovering, understood?"

"Yes."

"Actually, they change the word to *recovered*. So apparently you've made tremendous progress . . ."

"Yeah."

". . . in the time that you've allotted yourself. And again, as your little friend there says—look how far you have come. She says to sit back and look at all of it as part of *your* spiritual experience. Apparently, from what you've gone through, that's going to give you the capacity to not only continue to help yourself, but to help others as well."

"Okay."

"So she really sees so much of it as a blessing in disguise. And they also spoke of you having drinking troubles."

"Yes."

"But . . . as they said, and I agree with them—cut yourself some slack from a realistic point of view. We've all used a drink to help ourselves feel better at one time or another. Sometimes, yes, we do turn to things that we feel will help. But when it becomes overwhelming—when it becomes a problem—that's when you have to snap to attention and cut it off."

"Right."

"Your 'band of brothers,' and the others there, tell me that you have progressed. You have made great strides. Don't give up on yourself, especially when you look back and are able to see how far you've come. Like they are all trying to do. Unfortunately, it's very easy to look at all the sadness and negativity, and let it pull you down. But as the little girl states, look at the progress that's been made. Here on the earth, in Purgatory, we have to experience an equal balance of good and bad. If life were always a bowl of cherries, you wouldn't gain anything here. By going through the positives and the negatives, this is what's rounding us off, and making us the people we're supposed to be. They say that up ahead—and they don't mean by the weekend—it seems that eventually, you're in a learning situation where you're learning for yourself, but also helping others."

"Yes."

"And again, you'll be a great force and a great strength, because you've gone through it. Your little girl says that but for the short time that you knew her, she would not have experienced such joy if it hadn't been [for] you."

"Okay."

"And as she states, focus on that. Don't focus on feeling that you failed her or you're responsible for her death, or anything like that. It happened. Unfortunately, lots of people are very ignorant."

"Yes."

"They're not too fond of organized religion on the other side. Unfortunately, and I agree with them, in many, many ways, it's the world's troublemaker."

"Mmm-hmm."

"Even the little girl states that. Without telling me what, it does sound like she speaks another language. And even if it's not understood by you, you were still able to communicate."

"Yes."

"She says, and I think this is cute, she does admit to me—and it's in a very innocent way—she says she had a little crush on you."

(He laughs.) "Oh yeah?"

"Again, that's in innocence. You did look out for her. And she's just concerned from over there that so much has overwhelmed you that you're not giving yourself a chance to see all the positives in that bad experience. That's why I thought it was cute . . . I could feel her blush over there when she said she had a crush on you. So it's not surprising to hear that she states she's like a guardian angel around you. She states she has come in dreams . . ."

"Yes."

". . . but the thing she adds is that as long as the dream is a comforting visitation, it's real. If it's anything that upsets you, don't pay attention to it. She says your own mind can create anxiety in your sleep, so it's important to know the difference in a real visitation being a good thing. She knows you've had your days where you think maybe she's mad at you—she says that's completely wrong. And don't think that because they're over there that they don't get to say their true feelings. That's why your brothers over there, including your actual brother, state that if anything, they do feel a little frustration at your anxiety, because they already see the finished product. They see going through it all and what benefit it brought."

"Yes."

"Also, I did hear the name Mike, Michael called—they were also calling to Mikey, understood?"

"Yes."

"Usually when I hear a name called I assume the person is passed on, but in this case I think they are calling to somebody here on the earth. They give me the feeling there is significance there."

"Somebody who is here?"

"Yes. Somebody here on the earth that they are calling Mike, Michael, and somebody who even joked with me calling the name Mikey. There could be a Michael passed on, but there's definitely one here on the earth."

"Okay, yeah."

"One thing they bring up—you have kind of calmed down a great deal, yes?"

"Yes."

"Because again there's that ice cube over your head. Your brother puts it over your head, and says it's as big as the iceberg that sunk the *Titanic*."

(*He laughs.*) "Yes."

"But as he says, it's being done with humor, but also with joy and compassion. You've definitely cooled down and become more balanced . . ."

"Yes."

". . . and in harmony with yourself. And they all bring that up.

Their big complaint about you over there is that you think too much."

"Yeah."

"You're thinking too much. You're allowed to think, but you've got to give things equal time. If you only think about the sorrows and ugliness you went through, it's going to overwhelm you. And it's why they say don't be afraid when you're thinking to challenge the thought. As your little girl says, if you start to think about the negative that happened, you need to counteract that thought by thinking about the fact that you brought joy there—she was delighted to know you and have a little crush on you there, and you're not seeing it in that perspective. Even as your brother states, it's true—when we fall into depression and anxiety, it's not easy, and it certainly can take you for a wild ride. So you have to start to think about the joys that also came out of the same experience."

"Okay."

"I'll be honest with you—I grew up in a dysfunctional home. But I'll tell you the truth—I don't know what you've been through, but they've given me the impression that I wouldn't have been able to handle it, even with having been through dysfunction. I'm seeing the Cowardly Lion from *The Wizard of Oz*—you had to have had a tremendous amount of courage to get to the point where you are now.

(*Crying*) "Oh boy."

"Certainly the Divine Presence does send compensations and help in our difficult time, if we just take the time to look for them. You're not struggling alone. They from over there want to see you fulfill your purpose, your journey here. I'm not embarrassed, and I appreciate the fact that they tell me that I would not have been able to do what you've done. And I more than likely would agree with them. Especially when they showed me the military uniform. I know I wouldn't have been able to handle war, the military. That's why it never came to me. As your brothers say, these things came to you because you were courageously willing to take on those challenges, and deal with it the best you could."

"Yes."

"That's why they keep telling you to stop throwing so many good things that have come from a bad experience into the garbage with the bad. This has nothing to do with religion, but I saw Saint Teresa appear in front of me, and she brings the virtues of peace, strength, and endurance. But she also believed that everything is a grace. And that's what everybody over there who came to talk to you have been saying to me to tell you: that everything is a blessing, even if we see it as being heartbreaking, ugly, unpleasant, whatever. It still is a grace in one way or another. And even if you never really find out here its potential as a grace, one of these days you're going to go that way, and they state that you're going to be very happy with yourself that you took on courageously the challenge and survived it. You got through it. They are genuinely glad to be able to reach out to you. Even your buddies there—they crack me up because they keep saying, 'Whether he believes this or not, we're not here to preach.' Nobody's over there telling you to go to church every Sunday or anything like that. You have enough on your plate as it is. And I agree with them—for some people, religion doesn't have all the answers. Nobody knows best for you other than yourself. I also hear the name Mary or Marie. I don't want to be a smartass but everybody knows a Mary passed on."

"Oh, okay. I think . . ."

"It's too common a name, so I'll leave it with you. Even if you don't know right now, I'm sure you'll find one. Also, without being alarmed, your grandparents over there do bring up concerns with your dad's health. Not only in the physical sense, but emotionally. He's lost a son, he sees what you've gone through—even if people suffer in silence, it still will rattle their cage. It's almost as though I see you in a hospital. So at some point you may have been hospitalized."

"Yes."

"But again, you survived it. You're where you are. There is nothing wrong with being pleased with yourself with what you have accomplished. Being humble is swell, but you also have to give yourself credit when it is due. Don't tell me what it is, but the little girl gives me the impression that her name is something I have never heard before."

"Okay."

"The problem is that if my brain doesn't recognize, it would be like if she was speaking Chinese to me. I'd say I hear her speaking another language, but I don't know what she's saying. She gives me the impression that I wouldn't be familiar with her name, her culture, that sort of thing."

"Right."

"Also, I heard the name Charlie. Understood?"

"Yes."

"And you know who it is."

"Yes."

"He's passed on."

"Yes."

"He comes to you as family. I don't know if he means by blood, marriage, term of endearment. He also counsels you. He gives me the impression that you need to take your time with things. You aren't the most patient guy with yourself—everything has to be done yesterday."

(Laughs) "Yes."

"You just need to walk the path with the Divine Presence and take your time. He also expresses tremendous pride in you and the person you've become."

"Okay."

"Your brother spoke about animals that passed, too."

"Yes."

"He refers to them as children—part of the family."

"Uh-huh."

"And he states that when he first passed on—he admits he was kind of rattled. He's not in the right frame of mind, there is the element of fear and all, and he said the animals came to him first, and that made everything okay. Because what do animals do? They make you feel good. People feel safe and secure with them. He says that he followed them to what we would consider a rest home, and they go to sleep to give him the idea to sleep and rest for a while. The animals are always a genuine source and exchange of love. Also, your brother brings up that you might have seen him—like out of the corner of your eye."

"Yes."

"He tells me it was the real McCoy."

"Okay."

"Again, it seems you've already had evidence from him that he's around, and this was just another. But he's just confirming that it was really true. Also, I hear the name Matt. Understood?"

"Yes."

"He comes to you as family, in an emotional sense. He certainly embraces you with love."

"Okay."

"And also, I'm sure it started happening already, but it seems to be that you'll be getting out more up ahead. Understood?"

"Yes."

"And it is encouraged. However, your brother says not to dive into the ocean, but wade into it."

(*Laughs*) "All right."

"It's interesting—your little girl has been taken under the wing over there by several of your family members who have passed on. Because you took her under your wing, and they know that will make you feel like a million bucks . . ."

"Yes."

". . . because you have been worried about her. There are people there of her own family, but it's kind of nice that your grandmother says that they've taken her under their wing, because you did that, and you gave them the idea that it would be a nice thing to do. Somebody over there said the name Duke. I don't know if it's a nickname, a pet's name—I don't know. I don't know what to do with it, they didn't give me anything to go with."

"It makes sense."

"Okay, they're telling me that they have to pull back, so I guess I have to listen to them. But your brother, your grandparents, and the different people who are here certainly embrace you with love. Never feel alone, because they are always with you. And also your little girl does the same—she embraces you with love. They tell you to give yourself a couple of days with this, and then revisit it and allow what they've told you to absorb. With this they tell me they have to pull back. With that, they send love, ask you to pray for them, and with that—there they go."

I have to be honest and completely candid in the wrap-up of this story. Michael thanked us profusely for the session, and I know it did him a world of good. He was in such good spirits—no pun intended—that day after the session. I know he called his mom, and they talked at length. Things seemed to be on a great track, and the session really made a difference for him. But when it came time for the interview for this book, Michael bailed on us. Repeatedly. He set up times to be interviewed, and then disappeared. Initially we were surprised and disappointed—this was to be a story about hope, that anything can happen when we put our mind to it and that the souls are there to guide us. Isn't that lovely? How naïve we were. It's just not that simple. Not at all. People don't get better just because we will them to. Sometimes it's a process, and the process takes time. Recovery is a long road, and sometimes it's a matter of a few steps forward and a few steps back. Michael was ready to open his heart to the souls in the hereafter, and I'm proud of him for that. But he wasn't able to revisit the pain with us. I'm sorry for it, but I understand. It may have been too much for him to recount this story now. And that's okay. Our book deadline notwithstanding, Michael has the rest of his life to get well, to understand, and to make peace with his history. And his story is not for me or anybody else to throw on a timeline. Sally was kind enough, like she always is, to finish the interview with us. I can't tell you how grateful we are to a mother who loves her son, even though she was pretty damn sore at him for hanging us up. But she wanted to do the right thing for Michael and for us. Michael's story needs to be told, and it *is* a success story. We just have to look at success with a wider scope, and allow it to have its twists and turns.

We wrote to Michael after Sally's interview, letting him know he is a hero in our eyes, how proud we were of him, and how grateful we were for his story because it will help so many other people who struggle every day to survive. And because I believe there is good in everyone, no matter what the circumstance, like a little gift back to us—Michael responded with an apology that he just wasn't ready, and his thanks for our understanding.

9

ONCE
BEFORE
I GO

SHARON ROSE

We get many emails each week, from all over the world. Some are encouraging, some are helpful, some tell me I am going to hell for what I do, and some are really wonderful to read because they are filled with hope and the poignant stories of what people struggle through after loss. The emails represent all aspects of people's lives—their losses, their grief, and, in some cases, their hope.

The emails that are the most difficult to read often come in the middle of the night or in the very early hours of the morning, when people's troubles and heartache are keeping them awake. Many, many people ask me for the favor of a session, and that's where my heartache begins. Due to the nature of my brain and the toll the sessions take on it, the number of sessions I can do in a given week is limited. Between the clients who have paid good money to see me and the free sessions I do for people who have waited years on a list for the few spots we have every month, I am left with very little brainpower for any additional discerning. I've pushed myself hard in the past, only to regret it, so I have learned to be smart about these things.

Every once in a while, however, we'll get an email where the souls of the writer will literally crowd me to do something, *anything* for the writer. I read these emails hoping the situation won't be as dire as all that, but I know in my heart and mind that if they are writing in the middle of the night, there is something important that *somebody* wants to say. And because my duty is squarely with the souls, if they impress upon me to answer a letter, either with a personal note, a prayer card, or an additional session, then that's what I'm honor bound to do.

We received this email, and once it was printed and touched my hands, two souls, a male and female, immediately leaped out to me. I understand the circumstance far too well, and I understood immediately the souls' need to reach out.

Hello,

My name is Sharon Rose and I live in Virginia. I am writing because I have stage 4 cancer. I was diagnosed with breast cancer in 2007 and had a bilateral mastectomy. In 2012 we found that the cancer had metastasized to my liver. I have been on a variety of chemotherapies for 2^1/$_2$ years. What happens is that the chemo controls the tumors but eventually my body becomes resistant to the chemotherapy and I have to switch to a different kind. My options are becoming limited. Recently my oncologist tried me on Tykerb and I had a very bad reaction. We are now waiting for the last known drug for my condition, which is Xeloda.

Luckily the cancer is only in about 30% of my liver and I still have about 70% liver function at this time. Because of this I don't look like a cancer patient. But I have an extremely distended stomach, fibromyalgia, and severe arthritis caused by the medication. I sleep approximately 15-17 hours a day. My stamina is compromised. However, I have been lucky so far because the chemotherapy was working for me, and for the most part, my quality of life is good. Without chemotherapy, the cancer will spread rapidly and I would have 6-8 months. We just don't know.

But I didn't write to give you a history of my cancer. I am actually writing because I am terrified to die. Somehow, in my heart, I believe that I will not go to heaven. I was raised as a Christian and still hold Christian beliefs. But because of other interests in the metaphysical I feel like I have disappointed God and have not been obedient. Therefore, I am afraid that I will not go to heaven. I have interests that some Christians feel are forbidden. For example, my belief in Astrology. I sometimes find myself putting other Christians down in my mind because I think they are boxed into a narrow-minded understanding of the Christian faith. However, truth be told, I don't really know if what I believe is right either. I am afraid that I have not pleased God and that I have denied Him. I want to go to heaven more than anything in this world. I have had a very difficult life and I long for a safe, happy, loving, and beautiful place where my soul will finally be free. I have many family members and friends who have passed on already. I used to feel my mother's presence but I don't anymore.

My question is this—can George help me? I live on disability and I would pay Mr. Anderson if I could. I do understand

that charging for services is how he makes a living. But I
have thought and thought about who can help me with my
distorted beliefs and I cannot think of anyone besides George
Anderson. When I talk to pastors, they raise their eyebrows at
me. I read the book *George Anderson's Lesson from the Light*
and it was one of the most uplifting books I have ever read.

I guess I just want to know what the souls who have passed
on before me could tell me about my spirituality. Perhaps they
have some answers for me and maybe they could ease my
mind concerning my own death. Right now I would prefer to
go off of all chemo, but I am just too scared. I am just terrified
that I will not pass into an afterlife that is filled with love
and comfort. Is there any way that George Anderson could
help me?

I feel like George could help me with some of my fears and
insecurities. But I have no idea how open he would be to doing
this for me. More than likely the answer is no, but I thought it
couldn't hurt to ask.

Sincerely,
Sharon

I have always been particularly sensitive to people who are facing
end-of-life issues. I'm not sure exactly why, but I would put good
money on the fact that it's because of the fear. They don't know
when, they don't know how, and they wind up dying of fear just
as surely as they die of their illness. My young life was filled with

fear—I didn't know why the souls chose me, or why they talked, or why people here were afraid of it, or why they thought I was mentally ill. So I understand fear. And I understand the pain that comes with fear. Nobody in the end stages of life, with everything else to worry about, should also live in fear, not knowing what kind of peace and joy awaits them.

Unfortunately, sessions like these are not unusual. The difference here was that time wasn't the major issue. The last time I did a session like this, it was for a man who was only days away from passing from pancreatic cancer. I did that session at the urging of a good friend who knew the man's young family was terror struck at the notion of losing him. In that case, fear was also a factor—not so much for the patient, surprisingly, but for his family. I walked into his hospital room to see two young children, and it was easy to read the fear in their eyes. I knew that appealing to their sense of adventure and a clear plan of where their dad would be going would help ease that fear, and it did.

I decided that helping Sharon understand that all is more well than she realizes would make the rest of her time here easier, and help make her transition, when it happened, much more peaceful.

This is Sharon's story, in her own words:

My dad was a doctor in a very small community, and my mom was a stay-at-home mom. My dad was very powerful in our town, and there was always an issue of keeping up appearances for my parents. They had a very strong Christian ethic, but somehow that didn't really translate to love within the family.

When I was a little girl of about five years old, growing up in the 1960s, I was by myself a lot. I had brothers and sisters, but our ages were so spread out that I found myself alone most of the time. I was outside playing, and I remember looking up at the sky and thinking, *I want to go back—I want to die and go back to heaven.* All my young life was infused with the idea of *going back*—I didn't want to be here.

The most important memory I have of my dad is that I always wanted to be close to him. I really, really wanted to matter to him, but I felt like he didn't really want to be close to me. So I was always a little afraid of him. I know that as a doctor his job was extremely stressful, so I think when he came home, he took all that stress out on his kids. Even at a young age, I felt the tension in my parents' marriage and my dad's lack of caring for the family. I remember once, many years ago, my dad started a fire in the fireplace, and I was so excited about it. I had a blankie at the time that I always carried around with me. When the fire got going, my dad snatched the blankie from me with no warning and threw it into the fire. I was devastated, thinking, *Why would he do that?* But it seemed to be like that all the time—I would live in fear of his anger if I did anything, even something as trivial as spilling my milk. The fear continued as I got older. I had low blood sugar, and one night when I was told to set the table for dinner my hands were shaking. He became enraged and accused me of being on drugs.

I never felt good enough at anything I did because my parents were quick to condemn and very stingy on praise. I was always good at art and music, but I never got any affirmation from them for whatever talent I had. They just expected their children to excel at everything, and didn't see things like talent as a gift. There was never any acknowledgment.

My mom did occasionally praise things I did in my young life. She would compliment my piano playing, and she did encourage my artistic ability. She tried in her own way. I think she may have been a little afraid of my dad, but when it was just us, she was a lot more kind and loving than when he was around to see it. But my parents were still close, which was a weird dynamic—they had what looked from the outside like a solid marriage, but she never would step up or say anything to contradict my dad. Worse, however, was that she was never able to step in when she saw some of the terrible things my dad had done to me. When we were one on one, she was different. She made time for me and was very loving—but only when it was between us.

I was the second youngest of five children. I was very shy, and even at a young age I knew I had very low self-esteem. I never felt I was good enough. Ever. So by the time I was fifteen years old, I had started getting into drugs. I was also hanging out with people who did drugs. My sister was already in college, and even though I was younger, I hung out with her and an older crowd. I graduated from high school, but I got pregnant at seventeen. It was a very big disaster. My mother didn't cry—she wailed. My dad was so furious. You can't imagine how angry he was, and he said things to me that nobody should ever say to another human being. It was hell for three days. Within a week of telling them, they sent me to live with my aunt and uncle in California. So I had the baby, but when she was born, she had a congenital heart defect. Thinking back, I was so young, and so unable to make good decisions for her health and welfare. I felt I was at the mercy of whatever the hospital or doctors wanted to do. Her little body had to go through so many tests and procedures. If I had been older and maybe a little more able to assert myself, I don't think I would have allowed it, since she was so sick and seeming to get worse after every procedure. They tried to prolong her life, but they felt it was necessary to transfer her to another hospital much farther away. So from that point, I didn't get to see her a lot. It was very painful. But I did see her, and got to hold her, and I loved her very much—I wanted her. Everybody thought for sure I was going to put her up for adoption, but there was no way I was going to do that. I had turned eighteen before I had her, and people started freaking out that I had a legal right to keep her. That didn't go over well with my family, either.

She only lived for a month. But when she passed away, in my young mind it was sort of a relief, because I didn't have this big looming decision to make about her care and her welfare. The doctor was so cold, though—when he called me, he just said that my baby had *expired*. I didn't even understand what that meant—all I knew was that things like library cards expire, not people. Then I understood that she had passed away. We had a funeral, but my parents didn't come.

I was unhappy in California. I had never met my aunt and uncle before I was sent to live with them, and going from a pretty rural area to a place like California was, for me, like being sent to the moon. After my baby died, I knew I needed to move on somehow. I started my first year of college in California, just a few months after my baby died, I was a mess. I was still having post-partum depression and full of grief, and I had nobody to talk to. My parents didn't want to talk to me, and even my aunt and uncle distanced themselves from me, not wanting to get in the middle of everything. I felt completely lost. But my aunt and uncle decided it was best for me to go back to my home state to try to repair my relationship with my parents. So back I went to where I started.

Being back at home was horrible—my mother cried constantly and didn't want to talk about the whole episode, and my dad was mad all the time. All they wanted to know was why I had bothered to come back. I kept explaining to them that I was trying to make things right, but my dad was having none of it. After that, I distanced myself from them—I just stayed as far from my dad as I could. My parents decided that I was not going anywhere—I was to go to the college they chose for me, I would stay there for four years, and I would become a teacher. End of story. And that's what I did.

As soon as I graduated, I became what I like to call a college-educated runaway. I had a friend in Virginia, so I moved to a placed called Charlottesville—they have a big university there. It was in Charlottesville that I finally began to thrive. I worked for a while, and then got married at the age of twenty-five. Part of the reason I married this man was because he had a daughter, Amy, from a previous marriage. She was very young when we married, and although her mom was still around, she didn't have any real relationship with her. The marriage was not perfect, and we struggled financially, but Amy was a joy to me—she helped heal me. For six years she was my baby, and it was a wonderful time.

The marriage to Charlie wasn't working out, though. Before Charlie and I divorced, my parents had come out to see us. I remember they looked so different—they looked very happy. But instead of feeling happy for them, the anger and resentment of those young years started coming to the surface. I was angry that they were now so at peace, when they hadn't been like this when it mattered. But we had a good weekend. My dad on one day was watching me swim, and I found it very strange. Not creepy strange, but more that suddenly he seemed interested and focused on me. I felt in my heart that maybe for the first time he loved me. I wasn't sure, but I felt maybe he did. On their way home after staying with us, they were in a terrible car accident with a tractor trailer. My mother died within a few hours of the accident. My dad lived eleven days. It was horrible. Really, really horrible.

Of course I grieved—after everything, they were still my parents. About a year went by, and I found out that I had inherited money. Charlie and I were divorced by this time, but I had this incredible sense of freedom. For the first time in my life, I felt like I had options. I kind of developed a bit of an ego—which wasn't good or positive. I was never gorgeous, but I was attractive, so between my looks and my money, at twenty-nine years old, I pretty much got anything I wanted. I thrived on it, too. I decided to start traveling, which I did quite a bit of. I ended up teaching school in Grand Cayman. I taught special needs children who were pretty disabled. It was a difficult job, and it was sometimes hard to deal with. I found that within a short time, my drinking started to get out of control. I was already drinking when Charlie and I got married— more than the drugs that I had continued to do. But now, teaching in Grand Cayman, my drinking got out of control, and I knew it. I knew I couldn't stay there anymore—between drinking so heavily and being in another abusive relationship there, I knew I had to leave. I wasn't able to make friends easily because of my self-esteem, and I didn't have any real friends except for relationships that got abusive. So I went back to Charlottesville to teach again.

Shortly after I got back to Charlottesville, I was diagnosed with cancer. Breast cancer. I was forty-five, and I freaked out. I just freaked out—I did not handle it gracefully, I was terrified, I was angry, and I felt like after everything I had been through in my life, now *this?* I was really angry with God, and this is something I still struggle with—I cursed God. I was just so furious. I really headed downhill fast. Depression was always there throughout the entire history of my life, and I even felt depressed as a child. But this sent it downhill even faster. I was on some medication for depression, but it wasn't enough. I attempted suicide and other insane things. I was drinking heavily. I still was able to go through the motions—I had a mastectomy, and I went through chemo and then reconstruction, which did not go well. I ended up realizing I had to detox, and that I couldn't do it on my own. I went to a hospital to detox, but I ended up in their psychiatric ward. I was there for two weeks. I was a mess—I couldn't figure out anything anymore, and everything was so dark. I was running out of money, and I didn't understand how people just went on with normal lives when mine was such a disaster.

I remember sitting in the day room at the psychiatric facility, just not functioning. I had hit bottom. Hard. After two weeks, the doctors at the facility were still very concerned. I couldn't stay longer than two weeks, so they decided to send me to the Wellness Recovery Center in Charlottesville. I was scared, but it did save my life. The people there were wonderful. I stayed there for two weeks, and after that I was able to leave sort of resembling a person. I was still shaky, but I felt well enough to deal with the disaster my life had become on the outside. I was out of money now, and still having trouble coping. I was seeing a psychiatrist and a counselor, and they had me on a lot of medications; it took a long time to get the combination right. I was diagnosed with major depressive disorder, but I felt like I was able to at least resume my life now with the therapy and the right medications.

I tried working some part-time jobs, but I wasn't really doing well. I was going to Alcoholics Anonymous, though, and I felt good there. I loved it there. Sometimes I would go twice a day because I loved it so much. But I had to leave Charlottesville because it was an expensive place to live and I didn't have much money at all. I moved to a rural town not too far away that was much more affordable, and thought it would be a good place to continue healing.

Not too long after moving, however, my cancer metastasized to my bile ducts. I was in and out of the hospital because there were obstructions. I had surgeries and painful procedures, and it got really rough.

In 2012, I was diagnosed with liver cancer. I started getting worse, and not long ago, the doctor told me the right side of my liver is gone.

I am now terminally ill, and I understand that. And I need time to help heal myself emotionally before it's time to go. In some ways, it's a blessing to know that you have an illness that will eventually take your life. I know that sounds terrible, but anyone can die at any time, and some people don't have a chance to clean up their loose ends. So I feel like in some ways God has given me that chance. I know I have hurt people, said things I never should have said, and been toxic to some people in my life. It's almost like repeating the past—like instead of changing who I could be, I became what my parents were. I have issues to clean up, and the biggest one is learning to love people. I need to work on me right now, while I still have some time left, and be more loving. That's my goal at this point. And I have to learn how to forgive before I go. I don't want to leave the earth and go right back to where I started—it frightens me.

I'm afraid to go without being at peace in my heart, or knowing what is waiting for me when I get to the other side. I don't want there to be any pain, either physically or emotionally, anymore. I also want to repair my relationship with God, who I cursed and was so angry at for such a long time. I regret that. But I'm learning to love while I still can. I have a cat that brings me joy right now, and I'm developing some friendships and trying to deepen the relationships I have now. I still do my art, which is very healing for me—when I am doing my art, I feel like I am channeling the spirit of God. I feel really at peace then.

These days I feel really tired. I tend to isolate myself, but I'm making an effort to get out more, and have people over. I would like to volunteer for a little bit while I can. The depression is still here, so I have to be careful what I put on myself. I get wiped out very easily. There are good days and bad days. I'm only fifteen minutes from the hospital, and my oncologist is the best. Just a kind, loving, caring, and nurturing man. He treats me like gold. In a way, I feel like his caring and concern is a gift from God because I didn't get that from the other doctor in my life—my dad. He is a blessing in my life, and he is closer to me than my own dad ever was. The universe finally provided a caring, gentle man in my life. It's really miraculous in a way.

I'm a little afraid to move on. To the afterlife. I'm a little afraid because of the way I reacted when I was diagnosed, and that I may have ruined my chances of going back to heaven. I say "going back" because I feel like I've already been there. But I'm afraid I'll have to stand in place and atone for some of the things I've done in my life, and the people I have hurt. I've been reading a lot. I read George Anderson's books, and I read the Bible. I know that spiritual people say we all will go there, and that brings me comfort. I want that more than anything. I want to know I will be at peace when I die. It's my biggest fear—not being at peace when I move on. I admit I'm scared. But I pray a lot, and I'm working on trying to be a more loving person while I still have time. I have done the best I could—yes, I've messed up a lot, but I have to trust in what comes next. I have to learn to trust God and know in my heart that I am loved. Unconditionally. I don't think I was ever loved unconditionally. I want to know I have forgiven, and I want to know that I have been forgiven. But I need to believe that it will be okay. I just want it to be okay."

THE SESSION

"Okay, let's begin and see who comes to visit. Immediately a male presence comes forward—actually, three, and two females. Now, going on the assumption that he has to be somebody, a male presence comes forward, so I take it you understand."

"I understand so far."

"One male does come in a fatherly manner. Actually, another one did, too, so there may be more than one person who takes that role. Let her explain, but somebody comes forward as mother."

"Yes."

"I just wish they'd sort themselves out—I'm getting a lot of different signals. Yes, somebody comes to you as mom. She states she's the real McCoy, so that would mean she's your actual mother."

"Yes."

"Now, just so they don't feel I'm ignoring them, but there are also people around who are claiming they're grandparents, so I'm sure they're all passed on."

"Mmm-hmm."

"So they are near to you also. And also without explaining—
there was talk of a brother."

"Yes."

"Bear with me for a moment. There was talk of a brother, but
an actual brother to you . . ."

"Yes."

". . . who is there with them, but somebody else talked about
the loss of a brother, and then claimed he was the uncle. So I'm
assuming one of your folks lost a brother."

"Right."

"He's there also. But the actual brother comes to you as such, so
you yourself lost a brother."

"Yes."

"Okay, because there are two different souls saying almost the
same thing. Don't explain anything, but they tell me you're in a
rather awkward state, understood?"

"Yes."

"They give me the feeling that right now in your life you're between a rock and a hard place. Because I feel like I'm in a corner."

"Yes."

"You might feel right now that you are stuck. That you are
trapped."

"Yes. Very much so."

"I see Saint Barbara appear, who is the patroness of people who
feel trapped. She reaches out to people when they feel like they are
stuck. And I think in your case, that's why she's here and reaching
out to you. You feel you are cornered."

"I do."

"But your parents, your brother, these other people around you keep insisting that you know you're not struggling alone. They are certainly around you in a comforting sense, and they are doing the best they can to assure you that you aren't struggling alone. As your mom states, they can't interfere in your experience. And they tell me that what you're struggling with now is part of your life experience."

"Right."

"I also—again, nothing to do with religion—but I see Saint Teresa appear. Her belief was that everything that comes to us is a grace, whether it be positive or negative. Everything has some sort of purpose or opportunity for growth with it. So even if what you're going through now makes you feel stuck, you will find out later on—maybe not in this world—that it was a blessing in disguise. Your mom also brings up that you are frightened."

"Yes."

"And Saint Teresa appears again to tell you that there is nothing to fear but the fear itself. She states you're basically frightened of the unknown. Each day there's the fear that you don't know what's going to happen next."

"Yes."

"It's like me asking you to walk into a dark room, and you're frightened because you don't know what you'll find in there."

"Right."

"This came up from him earlier, but don't explain. When your dad made his presence known, he gave me the feeling that he feels he could have been closer to you."

"Yes."

"He brought it up before, I kind of forgot about it, and now he's bringing it up again and busting my chops, insisting I say it on his behalf. He doesn't come across as the mushy type . . ."

(Laughs) "No."

". . . because he says from over there, which you might find peculiar because of his personality, but just wanted to make sure you know he always loved you and he still does."

(Crying) "Oh, thank you."

"He's like me—he's not the touchy-feely type."

"Right."

"And also brings up that in many ways, a lot of what you've gone through in this life experience has kind of made you sick. Understood?"

"Yes."

"Your father also expresses regret that he kind of abandoned you."

"Yes."

"He was there and he wasn't there. And it doesn't look as though you grew up in a cherished home."

"No."

"And as your mother says, dysfunctional."

"Yes."

"And another reason why I'm being told by Saint Barbara that she reaches out to you so strongly—I mean she comes through in other sessions, too, but it's been a while [since] she's come through this strongly—is because ever since you were a child there was the feeling like you always felt you were in prison. You're in a dreadful situation you can't get out of, and you're stuck. Like being imprisoned."

"Yes."

"So she reaches out to you as sort of a guardian saint, so to speak. Okay, this is coming from her point of view, so don't read between the lines, but even your mom feels she could have been closer."

"Right."

"But it's the same thing—she hopes you know she always loved you and still does. I can say that at the time, when she was on the earth, she also felt she was neither here nor there. She kind of felt stuck as well."

"Yes."

"But she does give me the impression that you had a better relationship with her."

"Yes."

"She did the best she could. And again wants to make sure you know that she always loved you and still does. But again, with her I feel that when she was here she was trying desperately to be the heart and soul of the home."

"Yes."

"I don't know what manner he means this, but your father expresses regret that he was abusive to you."

"Yes."

"And your mom was trying her best to keep things together. But she admits from over there that a great many of the things that had gone on while she was on the earth she honestly did not know."

"Okay."

"But she and your dad did have a good relationship."

"Correct."

"But not so much with you."

"Correct."

"I feel like I'm worn out from the yelling and mental abuse—all unpleasant things."

"Mmm-hmm."

"Also—it's interesting—Saint Barbara claims you are a victim. I don't know what that means, but do you understand?"

"Yes."

"And from that—from that remembrance of being a victim, you made yourself sick. Understood?"

"Yes."

"There's just this feeling that you were made to feel so bad about yourself. And you've made yourself sick because of it. It's almost as if you feel you deserve it. And [that] throws everything in your life out of orbit."

"Yes."

"They talk about you having health trouble at this time."

"Yes."

"And this is not a cold. It's not like in ten days you're going to feel better. But as the saint states, it's as though part of you is afraid to love yourself, do you understand? It's like in many ways, because of your upbringing, you've been brainwashed."

"Uh-huh."

"It's like somebody has tried to make you feel like you are not a good person. And this is all coming apart in front of me, symbolically like a tornado hitting the room and ripping everything apart. It's like because of that, everything in your life has come apart."

"Yes."

"This is very sad to have to say, but I can definitely feel from over there that your dad feels embarrassed. He feels embarrassed and ashamed. Even when he was coming through, it's as if he had two feet in one shoe—it was very awkward. But somebody there told him to speak now while he has the chance, in order to close all those gaps. Your dad wants you to understand within yourself that you truly didn't deserve what happened to you in your upbringing. In many ways you were a victim of circumstance."

"Yes."

"Also, your brother claims to be around you as a guardian angel from over there. He also admits that he was not a very happy person on the earth. It's sad—there's so much scattering in your family—not that they're moving around, but it's more like the *Titanic*—every man for himself."

"Yes."

"And that is a very dreadful way to grow up. And a very frightening way to grow up. The souls say that fear is the worst of the negative vibrations, because all other negative vibrations stem from it. Also, there's talk of drinking troubles, too."

"Yes."

"I don't know who, and don't say—but either your dad or somebody in his family—there's a history of that."

"Yes."

"And naturally that doesn't help things either. Your dad says he also didn't have an easy upbringing here either. Not that he's copping out, but in a lot of ways, he didn't know any better."

"Right."

"He talks about night raids, and being frightened all the time as a kid. He also went through a lot of frightening experiences growing up."

"I didn't know that."

"But you grow up losing the ability to trust and feel stable. You could feel that one day you have the greatest family in the world, and then the next day, the you-know-what hits the fan . . ."

"Right."

". . . so there's no solid foundation of security. Very unbalanced. And your mother doesn't want to come across as a big crybaby, but she admits that when she was here on the earth, she also experienced a dreadful series of disappointments. Things started out differently for her, and then ended up where she would not have thought that would happen."

"Right."

"Like your mom says, you don't really know somebody until you live under the same roof with them."

"Right."

"And you have to give her credit—she's sincerely trying her best to keep everybody happy. She wants to make sure you understand that she knows she should have been more protective of you, but in many ways, she didn't know."

"Right."

"And your dad—now that he's in harmony with himself over there—which he had to do himself, he tells me he's glad to be out of here—away from the earth. I didn't have to live with him, but I can't say that I don't feel sorry for him, because his upbringing was very unhappy, too."

"Yes."

"He tells me that when he was on the earth, he suffered from an illness, and the illness was anger."

"Oh my gosh."

"I feel from him that when he was here, his anger level is abnormally high."

"Oh my gosh, yes."

"I can't say I don't feel sorry for him. I think that's why he's making such a big effort to communicate to you and apologize, and to let you know that he's finally at peace with himself. But that didn't happen overnight for him—he had to work at it in order to reach that point. But [it] just seems when he was on the earth, you'd want to ask him, *What the hell are you so pissed off about?*"

(Laughs) "Yes."

"Not that he's trying to make light of anything, but he jokes with me that when he was here he always seemed to have *a hair across his ass.*"

"Yes."

"And also, sadly, in life he was kind of a jealous man. The grass always looked greener in the other guy's yard—and he's not getting any breaks."

"Yes."

"So there's a lot of the youngster still in him when he was on the earth, even when he was grown up that was just like this angry child."

"Mmm-hmm."

"A lot of times your mom tells me she had to be kind of a referee, to try to keep things together. It wasn't like it is today when you could pack up and leave. In those days, things were very different. Without being alarmed, your mom is cautioning you to watch your step when you are walking. Especially on stairs. There's just this feeling that sometimes you get a little lightheaded."

"Yes."

"Your mom also reaches out to you in a comforting and compassionate sense—she knows you're ill presently, and she knows you're suffering. And again, you're in that all too familiar place within yourself where you feel like you're in prison."

"Yes."

"She knows you're doing your best to hang in there. But a lot of your worry is coming from fear of the unknown. Saint Barbara appears again to let you know that there is absolutely nothing to fear. But she's also down to earth enough to understand that it's easier said than done. Saint Barbara also came from having an abusive father, so it makes sense that she draws so closer to you. But again, she's coming to you with feelings of protectiveness over there, because even though you're not well, you're more scared than anything else."

"Yes."

"It's just that fear of the unknown. The souls know all of us are going to pass. It's not something we should fear. But the souls tell me you are very ill right now."

"Yes."

"So much of it, they say, seems to stem from your emotional and mental state. Not that you're a nut, but there's so much buried anxiety, and you do suffer from depression. And those things are absolutely illnesses. And can they kill you? I absolutely believe they can."

"Right."

"Your family over there states that they know you are going to pass on. But they assure you that you're not going to go until you're supposed to be there. And they know you are desperately trying to get well and stay well."

"I'm doing everything they're telling me to do."

"Exactly. Your father states that once again, fear has taken over. So if the doctor told you to put a bone through your nose, you'd think about it."

(Laughs) "Yes."

"They certainly tell you to pray to the souls and ask them for help—to help you to help yourself. But they reinforce that they cannot interfere in what is to be your life's journey."

"Okay."

"They bring up the loss of a child as well. Actually, they bring it up twice."

"Yes."

"All of a sudden your mom brings it up that she has grandchildren with her. One seems to have been before birth. There is talk of loss of a son, but they're saying it's before birth. There's talk of a daughter also."

"Correct."

"Your daughter—she did live here for a time, yes?"

"Yes."

"And she's telling me her passing has not helped your situation. It's sad to hear this, but she says your journey on the earth has just been a series of broken hearts. One after the other, from when you were born, to your young life, to losing her—she tells me you're the type that wants to do everything right, and the harder you tried, it seems the more obstacles appeared."

"Right."

"She does want to make sure you know she's all right and in a happy place."

"Good."

"And because she realizes you're ill also, if up ahead the time comes when it is time to pass on, she tells me she'll certainly be there to welcome you over."

(Crying) "Oh, wonderful."

"She hopes that as long as you know that, you won't be so frightened when the time comes. She says she's around you all the time. It seems you and she were close—she draws close to you now but does admit that at times when she was on the earth things could have gone better."

"Yes."

"Sometimes that's just the way things happen to be. But she speaks of a tragic passing."

"Yes."

"In the sense of her age as well as the circumstance. Be careful in your thinking, your daughter says. Because even with her passing, it's almost like subconsciously you convinced yourself that you deserved this."

"Yes."

"But she says you absolutely did not deserve this. She pays a compliment to you—she admires you that you're very persevering and you're very courageous."

(Crying) "Okay."

"Because in your life, so much *you know what* has hit the fan. It's almost as if at times you'd start to wonder *What the hell else is expected of me?*"

"Exactly."

"Now, she speaks of a pretty quick passing. She shows me a ball field, which is my symbol that this comes out of left field. And she brings up that she wants you to know that you did not fail here. Do you understand?"

"Oh, okay."

'Even she knows that you are constantly trying to do everything right. It seems you just reach that peak and then something else happens. It's sad to have to say this, but it's like your life has been a never-ending struggle. Where you are so at your wit's end, that frightens you also."

"Yes."

"Your daughter says you really need to sit back and pat yourself on the back. You've been through so much—but you're a survivor. You're surviving to the best of your ability. She tells me that you already know you're going to pass on, but in reality, we all know that—just not the day or hour. And she doesn't want you to feel that yours is an exception to the rule. We all will pass on in our own time. She's very near to you, and she really admires your courage and your perseverance. Not everybody could live through what you've gone through. And she knows that as long as you understand she's all right and that she will be there for you when your time officially comes. She'll be there when the time comes, and she says it's as easy as going from one room to the next. That's how easy and uneventful it is. But she'll be there to reach out her hand and guide you to the next dimension. And she hopes that just knowing that will take some of the bite off."

(Crying) "Okay."

"People are more afraid of the circumstances that will lead up to their passing than the actual passing itself. She speaks of you being seriously ill. To the point where it will eventually cause your physical death."

"Yes."

"Her first recommendation when you get there is to take an extended rest. You have gone through so much in your life, that the rest will reset and refresh your soul. You'll be whole again there. I just heard the name George, too. Somebody just came near to me here and told me he has the same name as me."

"Yes."

"He comes to you as family in some manner, and also embraces you with love."

"Wow, okay."

"He wants to reach out to show you how far he's come in the hereafter. Also, your daughter speaks of her father. I don't know how she means this, but she says she's with him. I don't know if she means she's with him over there, or she's with him on the earth."

"Okay."

"Also she says that things could have been closer in that relationship as well."

"Yes."

"Even with her father, you had kind of a tough go in the relationship, yes?"

"Yes."

"Again I'm feeling that abusiveness again. You know, I think the worst of your abuse has been mental and emotional. It's as if people have tried to convince you things happened and it's all your fault. It's just creepy. You're hit with it so often that you almost start to believe it's true. And it is not."

"Yes, okay."

"Your daughter does bring up that there's a huge part of you that wants to get the hell out of here."

"Yes."

"I see her gesturing where you put your hand under your chin and say you've had it up to *here*. But as she says, when the time comes that you get there, you will realize that you actually had a fulfilling life to the best of your ability here. And you did accomplish what you needed to. Her passing didn't help you either, and she knows that's the icing on an already rotten cake."

"Yes."

"But she thanks you for praying for her in your own way. And she says that sometimes you feel like you don't get enough signs from her. But your soul knows she's around, and that prompts you to speak to her."

"Yes."

"She talks about her passing being sudden. But she also says she knew she was going to pass on. I hope you understand that, without telling me anything."

"I do. Yes."

"So she knew. Now here's somebody who is close to you from over there, who also reaches out to you closely from over there, who has herself already gone through the transition. So here is somebody who is speaking from experience about how easy the transition actually is. She actually kind of kids you a little bit because she knows you're a little afraid."

(Laughs) "Really."

"She's not being insensitive—she just jokes that you're afraid of something so simple. She's been through it, and she can tell you how peaceful and beautiful the experience is. But she also knows that until you go through it for yourself, you're still going to have your fear and anxieties."

"Yes."

"She tells me that when she first got there she actually thought she was dreaming."

"Oh wow. Yeah, that makes a lot of sense."

"She talks about passing in kind of a sleep state, and she doesn't even realize it happened. Also she brings up to watch where you're walking. She says the illness is affecting your sense, but she also says you may have a tendency to see double. This all has to do with the illness. Her main concern is that you try not to think so much. The fear has been the danger factor in 99 percent of your entire life."

"Wow. Yeah."

"It's just—she's very happy there, but sometimes she just sobs for you because you've always been frightened. Ninety-nine-point-nine percent fear—from when you were a little girl, throughout your young life, through your marriage, the loss of your daughter—it's like you don't trust joyfulness. It's like if you let down your defenses and trust that things will be okay, that the other shoe will drop."

"Correct."

"It's all been part of the life experience. Yup, it's going to come to an end one of these days, and then you'll be able to seek out and find complete understanding of it, and earn the reward for having lived through it. She says there's even days when you doubt there's any world hereafter."

"Yes."

"But she says, heads or tails, you win. She'll be there to welcome you over, and she'll take you by the hand and cross you over. You probably won't even realize it happened. And because they know over there that sometimes illness of the physical body can affect the spiritual body as well, she recommends rest once you get there. She also talks about the animals that passed."

"Yes."

"Your other children, so to speak. A lot of them were there when she passed over, and greeted her. She speaks about working with animals over there, which I'm always glad to hear, and working with animals here that have been abused or mistreated, where she tries to work it from over there that somebody will come to their rescue. She makes sure they have a chance to get rescued and find a happy home."

"That's great."

"She speaks especially about cats. And it seems even in your life, animals have been tremendous therapy for you."

"Yes."

"A lot of times that's what got you through life. The concern for the animals' benefit and welfare."

"Yes."

"Your daughter tells me she's come in dreams. She certainly has been near to you, especially lately. Whether you are aware of it or not. She also says in regards to her passing, and she wants to make sure you understand this—no one is at fault and no one was to blame. Understood?"

"Yes."

"She wants to make sure you know that the only thing that separates both of you is *form*—the physical world. Naturally you'd rather have her here, but since that's not the way our life experiences work, when you go there, you'll understand better when she says to you that she's closer to you than you can imagine. When you go there, you'll understand it for yourself. They can be closer to us than anybody in the physical world. She does tell me this, and she's not telling you how to feel, but she promises you that you'll be very glad to be the hell out of here, too."

(Laughs) "No doubt."

"But even when that happens, she doesn't want you to lose sight of the fact that in this existence, you were a survivor. She knows there have been times in your life where you wish you could just die, but now that it seems to be knocking on your door, you're thinking twice about having invited it over. But that's just the natural path of life. She brings up a good point—because of your illness, there is a tremendous sense of liberation, understood?"

"Yes."

"I mean, she knows some days you feel like you got short-changed, but you also know that you are moving ahead and away from this life existence. And just the fact that you'll be reunited with her will be a big bonus. Her, the animals, and the people who love you. She also wants you to know that she did not suffer prior to her passing."

"That's good to know."

"Saint Joseph appeared in front of me, and he's the patron of a happy passing. That symbol backs up what she just said. Even though at first she thought she was dreaming, the pets helped to put her at ease. There was no fear at all."

"Good."

"I just heard the name Helen. And she does come to you as family."

"Yes."

"There's a motherliness with her. Like an aunt, grandmother—something like that. She says she's very close to your daughter over there. And she's taking good care of her. Your loss on the earth was definitely her gain in the hereafter."

"Awww. Good."

"She and your daughter are good pals. Also, I heard the name Rob or Robert. He isn't sure you'll remember him."

"I have to think about that."

"I'll just leave it with you. You can't remember everybody you ever knew in five seconds. But he's there and just reaching out."

"Okay."

"It's funny—you had cats."

"Yes."

"I know because my own cats are here sitting next to me, and your daughter is just delighted with them. This could be symbolic, but I just saw Saint Francis of Assisi appear, and the saint does compliment you on your kindness to animals. That you have been very kind to animals."

"Yes."

"He doesn't just show up because you adopted a goldfish. He blesses you for going out of your way for animals, and for your kindness even throughout so many episodes in your life. Especially strays. You've been there for them."

"Yes."

"And all of these kindnesses are remembered and stored in the memory bank over there. So, you'll get to benefit from all the good work you've done for them over here."

"Thank you."

"As much as your life has been 99.9 percent fear, we here are the heroes and heroines who come into this dimension and still try to do good despite terrible things that happen. But everything you have been through will eventually have purpose, meaning, and even joyfulness behind it when we get to the world hereafter. Even if it was unpleasant. You are gaining the spiritual rewards you earned as a soul on your own unique journey. Don't correct me, but I did hear the name Charlie."

"Yep."

"Let me explain—it can be somebody here, but it has to be somebody significant."

"Charlie is here."

"Okay, but significant?"

"Yes, very."

"Okay—somebody from over there called to him. Somebody close to him passed on knows him and can use you to reach out to him. And if you feel he can deal with this, and they do give me the impression you know who it is he is reaching out to . . ."

"Yes I know who it is."

". . . but once they know you know who it is he is trying to reach out to, then I don't have to work so hard. As long as the message is given to him that this individual calls to him with love."

"Okay, I can do that."

"The soul is thrilled now with that. It does feel like a female."

"Yes."

"There's just a nice comforting feeling with her. But she says she's around him, which I'm pretty sure is going to put a smile on his face."

"Oh yes, for sure."

"And she does bless you and thank you for delivering the message. But I think for the time being, Saint Barbara, who is still here, is certainly somebody you can reach out to in order to help you to help yourself."

"Okay."

"The souls tell me they're pulling back. Well—your dad says it anyway—he says he always loved you and he still does, even if he had a very strange way of showing it."

(Laughs) "Yeah."

"But he feels he needs to hear it, and it's also to redeem himself. So that you both can start out from a fresh place when you see him again in the hereafter. Your mom also embraces you with love, along with your daughter and brother. They ask that you remember to pray for them, and again—when your time comes, they will be there to welcome you over. Your daughter especially. She says don't be afraid—when it's time, and you feel it's about to happen, just count to three—one, two, three—and then just release. She says you'll be glad you did."

"Okay."

"But you know that already. But with that, they pull back, embracing you with love, until you see them again. With that they sign off, and . . . there they go."

I'm very proud of the souls in circumstances like this one—they line up like soldiers and put the past squarely behind them in order to help the people they love. There was a lot of ground to cover, but they did an amazing job trying to both take responsibility for the past hurt, and to pave the way for a new, bright beginning for all of them. Hindsight is an amazing thing, whether it happens here or hereafter—it allows us to look at something without the filter of fresh emotion attached to it, and to really see not only our part of an issue, but how it was felt by the person at whom our actions were directed. When we are able to look at anything without the distorted lens of pain, we learn so much about who we are as people, and as souls on a journey. Part of this new understanding in the hereafter is the souls' journey to fix what they broke on the earth. Another part is the pure love they experience for those they may have wronged in the past. It's easier to forgive people when you know that due to their own hurts and fears, they were unable to function in a loving way. It's easier to understand them as people when they are honest and just tell us that sometimes it really is beyond their control, but they still take responsibility for it nonetheless.

Sharon is a remarkable woman, and I was very happy to meet her. Her willingness to let go of the past, to deal with the present, and to welcome the future, whatever it holds, was something that did my heart good as well. It seems as if her terminal illness gave her life—it gave her back the ability to love, to forgive, and to understand. I've often found that the most living anyone can do comes precisely when we learn that life isn't forever, and tomorrow is not a guarantee. Sharon took this last, final lesson and made it a beautiful tribute to her own life. She is a real testament to the fact that peace is healing, and love does truly fix all.

On April 2, 2016, Sharon Rose lost her battle with cancer. In the last message we received from her, she told us about the disappointing diagnosis and how it was time to prepare for her transition. But she was calm and in a place of real understanding. She told us the words that would resonate in our hearts forever: "I am ready. I'm at peace." What a long road it has been for Sharon, and what an amazing transformation of belief she had. I hope she's now able to smile at the struggles she once endured and that she has found everything her heart yearned for on earth: happiness, love, and joy.

Epilogue

THE WHEEL OF LIFE

At the beginning of this book, we wrote that with every day that the sun rises, the souls have their hands and their hearts in our world, helping to shape the circumstances we live through. As our lives go on, and we struggle through difficult times and challenges, that statement has never rung more true. The souls have shown in so many ways their incredible influence in our lives, both on our plane and theirs. But why now? Why are the souls trying so hard to teach us that when it comes to life between heaven and earth, their ability to bring resolution and peace is unlimited? I suppose part of the answer can be found in the lives we live and the world we live in. Everything around us seems so uncertain in the circumstances we face and the struggles we endure. We are connected now on a global level that would have defied comprehension as little as twenty-five years ago, yet we have no more definitive answers about the nature of our spiritual journey now than we had then. We should know more, we should be more connected to our life's journey, and we should be less inclined toward the uncertainty that seems to permeate everything we know about the meaning of life. But we aren't. And I believe this is precisely why the souls have stepped up their communication to the earth, even in some of the more unusual circumstances they have come up against. But again, why now? I believe the rest of the answer is in the statement the souls have made to me in nearly every session since I began hearing from them more than a half-century ago—"We are closer to you than you imagine."

It is always gratifying in a session for the client to hear their loved ones state that they are much closer to us than we can imagine. I used to believe that the statement meant only that the souls were with us when they were needed, and that they cling to us in order to help us through our existence here. But the true meaning of that statement goes way beyond my simple understanding, and the souls have only recently begun helping me to fully understand. It may be that I have grown enough in my own education about life here and hereafter, or that we as a people have grown enough to understand more. It may also be that the souls trust us to know that not every circumstance of living and dying is perfect, even if the result eventually will be. And just because their world is perfect, does not mean it is not also a work in constant progress. They know that sometimes the road to peace may take a detour. They know that sometimes we will walk through many doors before we find the one we were meant to pass through. And the souls certainly know that sometimes where we start is not where we will end, no matter how well planned the journey was supposed to be. They know that life both here and hereafter will change many times until it brings us to our perfect destiny. The souls are closer to us than we imagine, because they *are* us. Let me explain.

Long Island, New York, in the 1950s was a very different world than it is today. It was a world away from the city life of the Bronx that my parents knew—but the promise of a new and happy life drew them and so many others to what was then a vast, open place where they could live out their lives as they pleased.

My parents were very frugal people, but when it came to the Church, money was *never* an issue—they gave freely, and in whatever way they could. When Saint Anthony's parish had its annual carnival, my parents packed us into the car to go and support the fund-raising efforts. As a kid, it's never hard to be dazzled by how an ordinary parking lot could be transformed into a land of magic filled with lights, sounds, smells, and excitement. My mother would do the exact same thing at every carnival: she would buy us three tickets each, which would entitle us to go on the rides she preapproved—the Whip, the Tilt-A-Whirl, and the magnificent Ferris wheel. During one carnival, I found myself wandering around, bored, having dispensed with my tickets in pretty short order. My father was making his way to the Church Hall, where they had a makeshift casino, and sensing that there was nothing better for me to do at this point but get lost or in trouble, he took my hand and led me into the hall.

The hall was filled with smoke and gaming tables and people gambling in the name of God. It all seemed so adult to me—there were people sitting and intently looking at the hands they'd been dealt, others watching the tables, and men carefully dealing cards and counting wads of dollar bills. My father took me by the shoulder and directed me to the roulette table. I got some disapproving stares from the people who were seated at the table, but my father once again put his hand on my shoulder and announced, "The boy is with me," and that seemed to disperse the scowls of the onlookers.

"No more bets, please." The wheel spun around in a dizzying

flash of colors and numbers, and the dealer gingerly tossed the ball into the wheel. I watched it bounce around, spin, bounce again, taking what seemed like forever to make up its mind where it wanted to be. Finally, it landed. "Fourteen black," the dealer announced, to audible sighs and one shrieking woman. The dealer placed more chips next to the woman's. She snatched them up in a flash and shouted, "Thank Jesus!" Watching her disappear from the table seemed to cause the dealer some discontent—I suppose that at a fund-raising event, grabbing your chips and going home was not the name of the game. But away she went with her winnings, and away my father and I went from the gaming tables and back out of the hall to the clean, crisp summer air outside.

That night in my bed, I thought a lot about the woman and the roulette wheel. It seemed too odd and random to me—fourteen black, not twenty-one red or even the double zero. As the ball wound its way around the wheel, it seemed to bounce from place to place, not knowing where to make its home. And it found a place so solidly that the trip itself seemed almost destined to end exactly that way. At that young age, because of that roulette wheel, I started to understand that destiny is a journey. It is a spin on the wheel of life.

All of us are part of a roulette wheel when we are on the earth, and quite probably even in the hereafter. We start out spinning in one direction against the motion of the wheel of life. We bounce from circumstance to circumstance, seemingly at random, until we arrive at the place that we somehow fell into as resolutely as if we had been placed there by hand. Is it all that random, or are we meant to spin furiously past circumstances, trying some out, bouncing in and out of lives we could lead, until we fall into the lifetime we are supposed to fulfill? I believe, after so many years of hearing from not only the souls, but people who still walk the earth, that the answer is actually both—our lives are a random set of fixed circumstances. Where our ball drops is the place we were supposed to be, or the place we are supposed to go. It's our wheel of life, and we decide whether we stay to open that door or leave to pursue another. At the same time, our destiny puts before us the doors we are supposed to consider. In a universe filled with unending possibilities, where the parameters are set only by our willingness to live within them, we choose the door or we allow the door to choose us. But no matter how we choose, the choice is still ours to make. And no matter what, the souls will always be there to guide us gently to our perfect resolution.

As I get older, I am finding that the only hard-and-fast rule is that there really aren't any hard-and-fast rules. I've learned that we can look at anything—life, the hereafter, people, the souls—and fit them into a box that falls nicely into our little parameters of belief. But like everything else I have experienced, the souls and the world hereafter are not quite so fixed and understandable as even I may have believed. I was so young when I started hearing from the souls, and I think in my youth there may have been a certain amount of naïveté that made me believe it was all like a painting—we could spend years looking at the different shapes and colors, but at the end of the day it was a finished painting. But as I got older, and heard more stories from people who lived incredible lives on the earth, and continued to incredible circumstances in the hereafter, nothing about our world or theirs can be put into so tight a constraint as to say, "Here is the end of the experience— here are the corners of our understanding." It goes on—sometimes beyond our ability to understand. So we learn more, and we print another edition of the story of the world as we know it. As we continue living, we continue learning, and life continues changing.

I think back to those days, watching that roulette wheel go around and around, it occurred to me that my dad and I were the luckiest people at that table. My father, with one hand in his pocket, unconsciously jingling his change because no money would be spent on something as frivolous as gambling, and his other hand on my shoulder as we watched the ball dance, land, and delight exactly one winner. The rest of the gamblers left, telling themselves it was all for charity, but each of them wishing they had been that lucky winner. My father and I had no pony in that race—so whatever the outcome, we were just observers, and were just as delighted that it should be fourteen black or any other number on the wheel—our die was cast, and nothing about our circumstance changed. Others, proud of their charity yet dejected, saw a little bit of life change for them that evening. And the shrieking woman—well, she hit the jackpot. All of twenty-seven dollars.

Life, both here and hereafter, seems so clear to us when we are right on top of it, living it every day. But a few steps back from the table, the board seems more interesting, and the scene is a lot more compelling. We have no idea what will happen, no matter how carefully we have planned, or how fastidious we are in following the game. Life, in the end, will spin around and around, dance from circumstance to circumstance, and settle at the place it was meant to be.

Many of the stories we decided to include in this book illustrated things that I simply did not know were possible until the circumstance came up in a session, and the souls were able to shed light on it. Other than the Stillwells and their children's amazing story, which I first thought of as an otherworldly anomaly, I'm finding that as the souls get more up close, personal, and *honest* with the world they left behind, they can tell us how things may not always come to the "happy ending" we thought it would, or the "perfect passing" we were told there would be. At least not right away. Even the "complete understanding" we were promised when we think in flowery terms about the souls and their world can be subjective—it all seems to depend on what each of us needs to complete the journey of our lives. The truth is—and I guess I'm old enough and experienced enough to understand it—that the road to complete joy, understanding, and happiness is a bit of a bitch sometimes. It seems somehow to keep us just slightly off our game, so that nothing in our lives is ever a sure bet, and the only thing we can count on is ourselves, our ability to change with whatever comes, and our desire to be at peace with it.

So where does this all leave us? To be honest, I'm occasionally left scratching my head after a session, sometimes in amazement at the ingenuity of it all, and sometimes in absolute confusion, because it seems to me the hereafter may not quite have its act together like I had originally thought. The hereafter, it seems, is as human as we are—it moves on, it changes when it needs to, it gets a little stubborn, it resists a bit, but then it gives all it has to us. As we learn and grow, so does the world we hope to inhabit one day. I suppose it is a bit naïve to think that things are so well ordered everywhere but on the earth—hey, that's what I was also led to believe by the souls at one time, too. But I'm learning and understanding, and perhaps able to accept and grow from understanding, that the hereafter isn't some painting that never changes. The souls start to help me understand that the colors in the painting sometimes need to change, the shapes need to shift, the painting may have to get bigger to accommodate something unusual or shrink so as not to be too overwhelming for a soul. It lives, it breathes—it is as human as we are. Maybe not quite the "heaven" we thought it was—a lovely, static destination—but more a place where anything is possible and everything can happen for its own good—an unexpected but amazing journey.

"We are closer to you than you can imagine." From that simple statement comes a profound truth. The souls are just like us, and they always will be—they move, they change, and they grow. It's a nice thought. It takes so much of the odd mystery from a place that would seem daunting by anyone's standards. But it also makes it more *real* to us. And more attainable. One day, the wheel of our lives, both here and hereafter, will line up in spectacular fashion. The door we walked through and the door we were meant to walk through will meet each other in a beautiful place, and at the best time possible. We may walk in one door, get pushed through another, get pulled into yet another circumstance, and then guided to the best possible outcome, but it is all part of our beautiful journey on the earth, and also in the hereafter, where we continue to change the worlds we see simply by needing it to happen.

As the souls have told me many times in my life, the journey from earth to the world hereafter is like walking through a door. How right they were, and what perfect sense it makes. How naïve we were to only think it was one door, and in one direction. Now we know better. The souls have been there, and they will always be there. No matter what the struggle, the story of our lives will always have a happy ending. And it all started with our decision to walk forward on an incredible journey through a life on earth with a view toward heaven.